The Speaker's Quotebook

The Speaker's Quotebook

Stories, Illustrations, and Anecdotes

Benjamin R. De Jong

Baker Books

A Division of Baker Book House Co
Grand Rapids, Michigan 49516

ISBN: 0-8010-3030-7

Printed in the United States of America

FOREWORD

It has been my pleasure and reward to have my office next to Mr. De Jong. Many times I have been greeted with this salutation: "Mitchell, you ought to get a supply of this book for the students. I will encourage them to buy it because no student should be without it." Usually he was right, and the life of many a student was enriched.

In putting this material in book form, Mr. De Jong is only extending what he has done for many years. His constant witness in the pulpit, classroom, and the written page is evidenced by his large spiritual outreach. You will do well to read and use this book often. It will enliven your conversation and put you in quick contact with the hearer.

I heartily recommend this work to every pastor and Christian worker.

William Roy Mitchell, Business Manager
Grand Rapids School of the Bible and Music

PREFACE

This collection of quotations has been gathered from various sources over a period of more than fifty years. I used them in school publications when I was a principal in a Christian school. Later in my ministry I used them to spice my church bulletins.

Solomon says "A word fitly spoken is like apples of gold in pictures of silver." Many times a brief word fitly spoken can say more than many paragraphs of cumbersome words. May you enjoy reading and using these "fitly spoken words."

CONTENTS

One minute
of keeping your mouth shut
is worth
an hour's explanation.

BIBLE MATHEMATICS
We are not to add to the Bible,
nor to subtract from it,
but to rightly divide it.

The emptier the pot,
the quicker it boils.
WATCH YOUR TEMPER.

When it comes time to die,
make sure
that all you have to do
is die!

He that goes
a-borrowing
goes
a-sorrowing.

If you wouldn't write it and sign it, don't say it.

Withdraw thy foot from thy neighbor's house; lest he be weary of thee, and so hate thee (Prov. 25:17).

You have never tested God's resources until you have attempted the impossible.

What a splendid thing it would be if those who lose their tempers could not find them back again.

Make the most of life before most of life is gone.

A continual dropping in a very rainy day and a contentious woman are the same (Prov. 27:15).

If you think you are too small to do a big thing, try doing small things in a big way.

Whence came ye is not as important as whither goest thou.

Do what good you can today, you may not be here tomorrow.

The trouble with a lot of smart kids is that they don't smart in the right place.

Face powder can catch a man, but it takes baking powder to hold a man.

A word fitly spoken is like apples of gold in pictures of silver (Prov. 25:11).

Life is like a band—we need not all play the same part, but we must play in harmony.

You had better check up before you check out.

Three thoughts on conversation:
 Is it true?
 Is it kind?
 Is it necessary?

Do all the good you can
by all the means you can
in all the ways you can
in all the places you can.

The best safe for a man's money is a prudent wife.

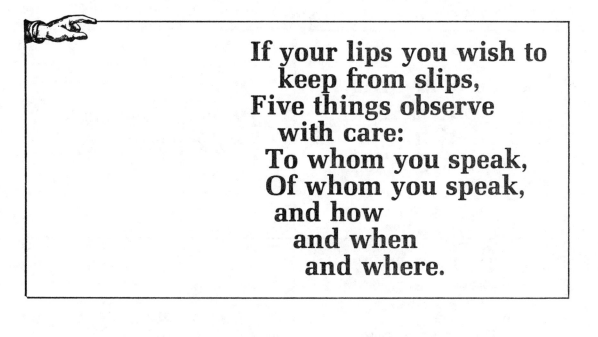

If your lips you wish to
keep from slips,
Five things observe
with care:
To whom you speak,
Of whom you speak,
and how
and when
and where.

● Do good with what thou hast or it will do thee no good.

● Don't make up your mind until you know the facts.

● Don't wait for the hearse to take you to church.

● You can never speak a fine word too soon, for you never know how soon
it will be too late.

● A good example is the best sermon.

Do not pray for easy lives;
Pray to be strong men.

We may have committed the
Golden Rule to MEMORY,
but what we really need to do
is to commit it to LIFE.

**Give every man
your EAR
but few
your MOUTH.**

*Plan your work—
work your plan.*

HOW TO WORSHIP
Be silent.
Be thoughtful.
Be reverent,
    For this is the house
    of the Lord.
BEFORE the service,
    speak to God.
DURING the service, let
    God speak to you.
AFTER the service,
    speak to one another.

*WILL POWER
is the ability
to eat
one salted peanut.*

**Three hints for making a speech:
  1 Be sincere.
  2 Be brief.
  3 Be seated.**

*When God bolts a door
don't try
to get through a window.*

Life by the yard is hard,
But by the inch, it's a cinch.
One step and then another,
Take thy way—live day by day.

Efficiency
Economy
Endurance
Apply these E's now.
They lead to EASE later.

**There's not a
RIGHT WAY
to do a
WRONG THING.**

2/3 of
PROMOTION
is
MOTION

*MUSIC LESSON:
Sometimes B sharp.
Never B flat.
Always B natural.*

**A FAULT-MENDER
is better than
A FAULT-FINDER.**

If I stop to think
BEFORE I speak,
I won't have to worry AFTERWARD
about what I said BEFORE.

Don't think people judge your generosity by the amount of advice you give away.

If you can't make light of your troubles, keep them in the dark.

We hear a lot of good mixers these days, but what we really need is more separators.

Change the contents of the heart and you will alter the droppings of the mouth.

Be sure you are right, and then go ahead.

Time may wrinkle the brow but should never weary the spirit.

There is only one thing to do about anything and that is the right thing.

If you don't say it, you won't have to unsay it.

Carve your name on hearts, not on marble.

Do unto others as though you were the others.

**OVERLOOK
the faults of others
but LOOK OVER
your own carefully.**

To stay youthful
stay useful.

If thou wouldst live long,
live well;
for folly and wickedness
shorten life.

Be humble
or you will
T
 U
  M
   B
    L
     E!

*Seconds count,
especially
when dieting.*

★ The kindness we resolve to show tomorrow cures no headaches today.

★ Smile a while and give your face a rest.

★ Some people would say more if they talked less.

Give God the blossom of your life; put Him not off with the fallen leaves.	Be at war with your vices; Be at peace with your neighbors.
If you have a half hour to spare, don't spend it with someone who hasn't.	Every day is judgment day—use a lot of it!
A pint of example is worth more than a gallon of advice.	Be the first to praise and the first to deserve praise.
Be slow in choosing a friend—slower in changing.	Whatever your lot, begin to cultivate it.

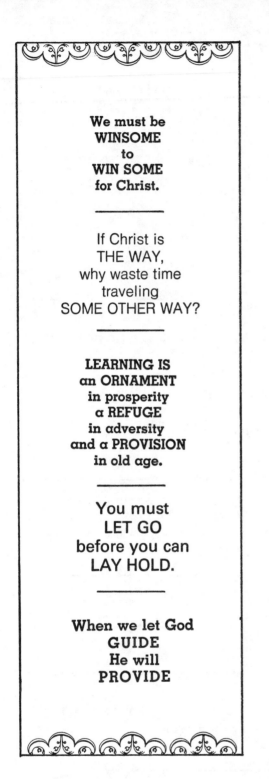

We must be
WINSOME
to
WIN SOME
for Christ.

If Christ is
THE WAY,
why waste time
traveling
SOME OTHER WAY?

LEARNING IS
an **ORNAMENT**
in prosperity
a **REFUGE**
in adversity
and a **PROVISION**
in old age.

You must
LET GO
before you can
LAY HOLD.

When we let God
GUIDE
He will
PROVIDE

If you want the world to HEED, Put your CREED Into your DEED.

A child of God should be serious without being sour, and happy without being foolish.

The teeth may be FALSE, but let the tongue be TRUE.

Don't tell me how much you know until I find out how much you care.

 Good advice is not better than poor advice, unless you follow it.

It is better to dwell in the wilderness, than with a contentious and an angry woman (Prov. 21:19).

A good place to find a helping hand is at the end of your arm.

YESTERDAY is a cancelled check.
TOMORROW is a promissory note.
TODAY is the only cash you have.
Spend it wisely.

A temper is a valuable possession, don't lose it.

When you meet temptation, turn to the right.

The best way to live in the world is to live above it.

Work is the best thing ever invented for killing time.

When the OUTLOOK is bad, try the UPLOOK.

I shall pass this way but once;
    any good that I can do,
any kindness that I can show,
        let me do it now,
for I shall not
    pass this way again.

Better alone than in bad company.

Beware of the barrenness of a busy life.

A smile is an asset,
a frown is a liability.

Walk softly.
Speak tenderly.
Pray fervently.

Never throw mud.
You may not hit your mark,
    but you will have
        dirty hands.

If slighted, slight the slight, and love the slighter.

If you are planning to do a mean thing,
wait until tomorrow,
If a good thing,
do it today.

TEN SPIRITUAL TONICS

1 Stop worrying. Worry kills life.
2 Begin each day with prayer. It will arm your soul.
3 Control appetite. Overindulgence clogs body and mind.
4 Accept your limitations. All of us can't be great.
5 Don't envy. It wastes time and energy.
6 Have faith in people. Cynicism sours the disposition.
7 Find a hobby. It will relax your nerves.
8 Read a book a week. It will stimulate and broaden your views.
9 Spend some time alone. It gives peace, solitude, and silence.
10 Try to want what you have, instead of spending your strength trying to get what you want.

—Feinberg

The only way to settle a disagreement
is on the basis of what's right—
not who's right.

———

**The question is not always where we stand
but in which direction we are going.**

———

A college education seldom hurts a man
if he is willing to learn a little something
after he graduates.

———

**What counts is not the number of hours you put in,
but how much you put in the hours.**

———

Your ulcers are not due to what you are eating,
but what's eating you.

———

**Any person who is always feeling sorry for himself,
SHOULD BE.**

YOU WILL NEVER BE SORRY—
For thinking before acting,
For hearing before judging,
For forgiving your enemies,
For being candid and frank,
For helping a fallen brother,
For being honest in business,
For thinking before speaking,
For being loyal to your church,
For standing by your principles,
For stopping your ears to gossip,
For bridling a slanderous tongue,
For harboring only pure thoughts,
For sympathizing with the afflicted,
For being courteous and kind to all.

THOMAS JEFFERSON'S DECALOGUE

1 Never put off till tomorrow what you can do today.
2 Never trouble another with what you can do yourself.
3 Never spend your money before you have it.
4 Never buy what you do not want, because it is cheap; it will be dear to you.
5 Pride costs us more than hunger, thirst, and cold.
6 We never repent for having eaten too little.
7 Nothing is troublesome that we do willingly.
8 How much pain have cost us the evils which have never happened.
9 Take things always by their smooth handle.
10 When angry, count ten before you speak. If very angry, count one hundred.

Staying calm is the best way to take the wind out of an angry man's sails.

If you are unkind, you're the wrong kind.

We cannot cause the wind to blow the way we want it to, but we can so adjust our sails that they will take us where we want to go.

Be not angry that you cannot make others as you wish them to be, since you cannot make yourself as you wish to be.

—Thomas à Kempis

THE EASY ROAD CROWDED

The easy roads are crowded,
   And the level roads are jammed;
The pleasant little rivers
   With the drifting folks are crammed,
But off yonder where it's rocky,
   Where you get a better view,
You will find the ranks are thinning
   And the travelers are few.
Where the going's smooth and pleasant
   You will always find the throng,
For the many, more's the pity,
   Seem to like to drift along.
But the steps that call for courage
   And the task that's hard to do,
In the end results in glory
   For the never-wavering few.

—Messick

DON'T LET YOURSELF . . .
WORRY when you're doing your best.
HURRY when success depends on accuracy.
THINK evil of anyone until you have the facts.
BELIEVE a thing is impossible without trying it.
WASTE time on trivial matters.
IMAGINE that good intentions are a satisfying excuse.
HARBOR bitterness toward God or man.

Always try to drive so that your license will expire before you do.	**Keep your fears to yourself, but share your courage with others.**
You can't be the salt of the earth without smarting someone.	As cold water to a thirsty soul, so is good news from a far country (Prov. 27:2).
Jumping at conclusions is not half as good exercise as digging for facts.	**A soft answer has often been the means of breaking a hard heart.**

TWELVE THINGS TO REMEMBER

1 The value of time.
2 The success of perseverance.
3 The pleasure of working.
4 The dignity of simplicity.
5 The worth of character.
6 The power of kindness.
7 The obligation of duty.
8 The influence of example.
9 The wisdom of economy.
10 The virtue of patience.
11 The improvement of talent.
12 The joy of originating.

GOD, grant me the
serenity to accept
the things I cannot change;
to change the things
I can;
and the wisdom to know
the difference.

Itching for what you want doesn't do much good — you've got to scratch for it.

It is not he who has little, but he who wants more, who is poor.

A little thing is a little thing, but faithfulness in little things is a great thing.

Dost thou love life? Then don't squander time; that's the stuff life is made of.
—Benjamin Franklin

Frugality is good if liberality be joined by it.

WAIT ON

To talk with God,
  No breath is lost—
Talk on!

To walk with God,
  No strength is lost—
Walk on!

To wait on God,
  No time is lost—
Wait on!

When we see the lilies
  spinning in distress.
Taking thought to manufacture
  their own loveliness.
When we see the birds all building
  barns for store,
'Twill then be time to worry
  —not before!

GIFTS
To your enemy, FORGIVENESS.
To an opponent, TOLERANCE.
To a friend, YOUR HEART.
To a customer, SERVICE.
To all men, CHARITY.
To every child, A GOOD EXAMPLE.
To yourself, RESPECT.

Four things a man must learn to do
If he would make the record true:
To THINK without confusion clearly;
To LOVE his fellowmen sincerely;
To ACT from honest motives purely;
To TRUST in God and heaven securely.
—Henry Van Dyke

A CREED FOR EVERYONE

SILENCE when your words would hurt.
PATIENCE when your neighbor's curt.
DEAFNESS when the scandal flows.
THOUGHTFULNESS for other's woes.
PROMPTNESS when stern duty calls.
COURAGE when misfortune falls.

WORLD'S GREATEST NEED

A little more kindness and a little less creed;
A little more giving and a little less need;
A little more smile and a little less frown,
A little less kicking a man when he's down;
A little more "we" and a little less "I",
A little more laughs and a little less cry;
A little more flowers on the pathway of life;
And fewer on graves at the end of the strife.

It is never the right time to do the wrong thing.

A single track mind is all right if it is on the right track.

A little explained, endured, forgiven, and a quarrel is cured.

Deal with the faults of others as gently as with your own.
—Henrichs

Conviction is worthless unless it is converted into conduct.
—Thomas Carlyle

A peck of common sense is worth a bushel of learning.

Speak kind words and you will hear kind echoes.

Whatever you dislike in another person be sure to correct it in yourself.

Instead of pointing a critical finger, try holding out a helping hand.

It's smart to pick your friends — but not to pieces.

Habit is a cable; we weave a thread of it every day, and at last we cannot break it.

BE SYMPATHETIC; you know it could happen to you.

The load becomes light which is cheerfully borne.

One thing at a time and that done well
is a good rule as many can tell.

**Let a pig and a boy have everything they want,
and you'll get a good pig and a bad boy.**
— Copeland

The Lord sometimes takes us into troubled waters
not to drown us, but to cleanse us.

I can alter my life by altering my attitude of mind.

If you can't make light of your troubles,
keep them in the dark.

OUR NEED

We mutter and sputter,
We fume and we spurt;
We mumble and grumble,
Our feelings get hurt;
We can't understand,
Our vision grows dim;
When all we need is,
A moment with HIM!

Is your place a small place?
Tend it with care—
He set you there.
Is your place a large place?
Guard it with care—
He set you there.
Whate'er your place it is
Not yours alone, but His
Who set you there.

HOW TO LIVE

Worry less and work more
Ride less and walk more
Frown less and laugh more
Drink less and breathe more
Eat less and chew more
Preach less and practice more.

—Excell

Fine eloquence consists in saying all that should be,
not all that could be
said.

Some women work so hard to make good husbands
that they never quite manage to make good wives.

It also takes two to make up after a quarrel.

If Christians do not "come apart and rest a while,"
they may just plain come apart.

—Havner

Every calling is great when greatly pursued.

SEE WHAT HAPPENS
Give God the first choice
of your time, your effort,
your thinking, and your money.
Then, see what happens.

Be patient with children—
You are dealing with soul stuff.

Children need models more than
they need critics.

If you confer a benefit,
never remember it.
If you receive one,
never forget it.

The chains of habit are generally too small to be felt until they are too strong to be broken.

Before you give anyone a piece of your mind,
You ought to make sure that you can get by with
what you have left!

You will never FIND time for anything.
If you want time, you must MAKE it.

The greatest thing in this world is
not so much where we stand as in
what direction we are traveling.

A new way to spell disappointment—
change the d to h and it will spell HISAPPOINTMENT.

Worry is interest paid on trouble before it is due.

If you want work well done,
Select a busy man—
The other kind have no time.

Building boys is better than mending men.

No wind can do him any good who steers for no port.

It's right to be contented with what you have but never with what you are.

It is better to look ahead and prepare than to look back and regret.

Learn from the mistakes of others, you cannot possibly live long enough to make them all yourself.

The secret of contentment is knowing how to enjoy what you have and be able to lose all desire for things beyond your reach.

Example is not the main thing in influencing others, it is the only thing.

The way to avoid great faults is to beware of small ones.

Folks who never do any more than they are paid for, never get paid for any more than they do.

It's what we learn after we think we know it all that counts.

The largest room in the world is the room for improvement.

An ounce of fact means more than a ton of argument.

— Martin Vanbee

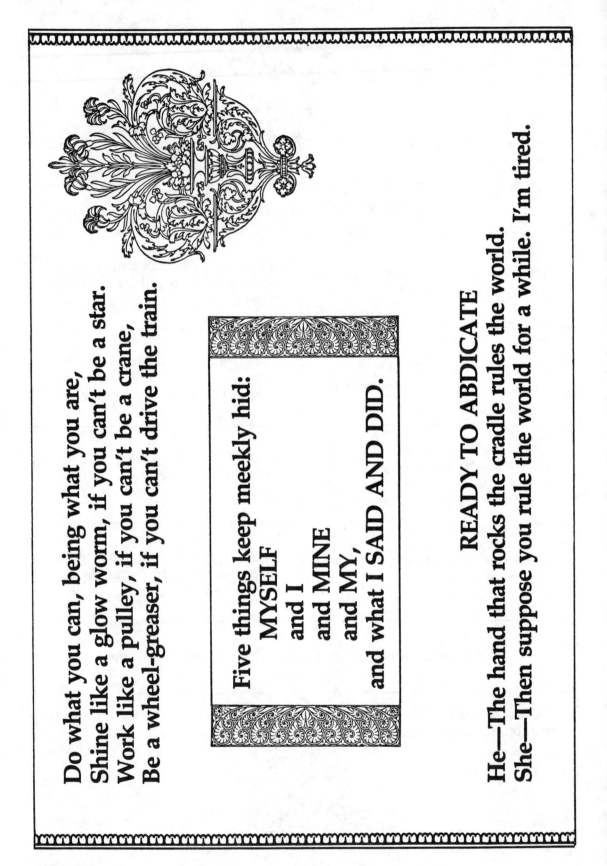

Do what you can, being what you are,
Shine like a glow worm, if you can't be a star.
Work like a pulley, if you can't be a crane,
Be a wheel-greaser, if you can't drive the train.

Five things keep meekly hid:
MYSELF
and I
and MINE
and MY,
and what I SAID AND DID.

READY TO ABDICATE

He—The hand that rocks the cradle rules the world.
She—Then suppose you rule the world for a while. I'm tired.

AMBITION

It is not so much what we know as how well we use what we know.

Jumping at conclusions is not half as good exercise as digging for the facts.

No one is a failure in this world who lightens a burden for someone else.

All that is necessary for the triumph of evil is that good men do nothing.

Some people take a stand for Christ, and never move again.

He becometh poor who dealeth with a slack hand; but the hand of the diligent maketh rich (Prov. 10:4).

A virtuous woman is the crown of her husband; but she that maketh ashamed is the rottenness of his bones (Prov. 12:4).

If at first you don't succeed, try a little ARDOR.

The measure of your usefulness is determined by the measure of your consecration.

The lazy man aims at nothing and usually hits it.

The best way to get rid of unpleasant duties is to discharge them faithfully.

A good thing to remember,
a better thing to do—
work with the construction gang,
not with the wrecking crew.

Experience gained the hard way brings knowledge that remains.

No life can be dreary when work is delight.

You never know what you can do until you try.

The man who is waiting for something to turn up might do well to start with his own shirt sleeves.

EARLY RISERS

ABRAHAM *rose early to stand before the Lord. (Gen. 19:27)*
JACOB *rose up early to worship the Lord. (Gen. 28:18)*
MOSES *rose early to give God's message to Pharaoh. (Exod. 8:20)*
MOSES *rose early to build an altar to God. (Exod. 24:4)*
MOSES *rose early to meet God at Sinai. (Exod. 34:4)*
JOSHUA *rose early to lead Israel over Jordan. (Josh. 3:1)*
JOSHUA *rose early to capture Jericho. (Josh. 6:12)*
JOSHUA *rose early to take Ai. (Josh. 8:10)*
GIDEON *rose early to examine the fleece. (Judg. 6:38)*
HANNAH *and* ELKANAH *rose early to worship God. (I Sam. 1:9)*

It doesn't do a man good to sit up and take notice if he keeps on sitting.	I am not what I ought to be; I am not what I wish to be; But by the grace of God, I am not what I used to be.
Have your tools ready and God will find you work.	**How busy is not so important as why busy. The bee is praised; the mosquito is swatted.**
Human beings, like chickens, thrive best when they scratch for what they get.	Intentions, like eggs, soon spoil unless hatched.
If you want your dreams to come true, don't oversleep.	**You always have time for things you put first.**
Horace Mann once said, "I have never heard anything about the resolutions of the apostles, but I have heard a great deal about the acts of the apostles.	If a task is once begun Never leave it till it's done. Be the labor great or small Do it well or not at all.

Reaching one person at a time is the best way of reaching all the world in time.	Find out what God would thee do, And do that little well. For what is great and what is small, 'Tis only He can tell.
Isn't it true—you can usually do the things you want to do.	**Many people have a good aim in life but most of them don't know when to pull the trigger.**

We all can do more than we have done,
And not be one whit the worse;
It never was loving that emptied the heart
Nor giving that emptied the purse.

WANTED . . . MEN!

There is a story to the effect that a certain society in South Africa once wrote to David Livingston: "Have you found a good road to where you are? If so, we want to know how to send other men to join you. Livingston replied: "If you have men who will come ONLY if they know there is a good road, I DON'T WANT THEM. I want men who will come if there is NO road at all."

What a crying need there is for such men in the work of Christ today!

—Truth for Youth

HOW TO LIVE A HUNDRED YEARS HAPPILY

1. *Do not be on the outlook for ill health.*
2. *Keep usefully at work.*
3. *Have a hobby.*
4. *Learn to be satisfied.*
5. *Keep on liking people.*
6. *Meet adversity valiantly.*
7. *Meet the little problems of life with decision.*
8. *Above all, maintain a good sense of humor, best done by saying something pleasant every time you get a chance.*
9. *Live and make the present hour pleasant and cheerful. Keep your mind out of the past, and keep it out of the future.*

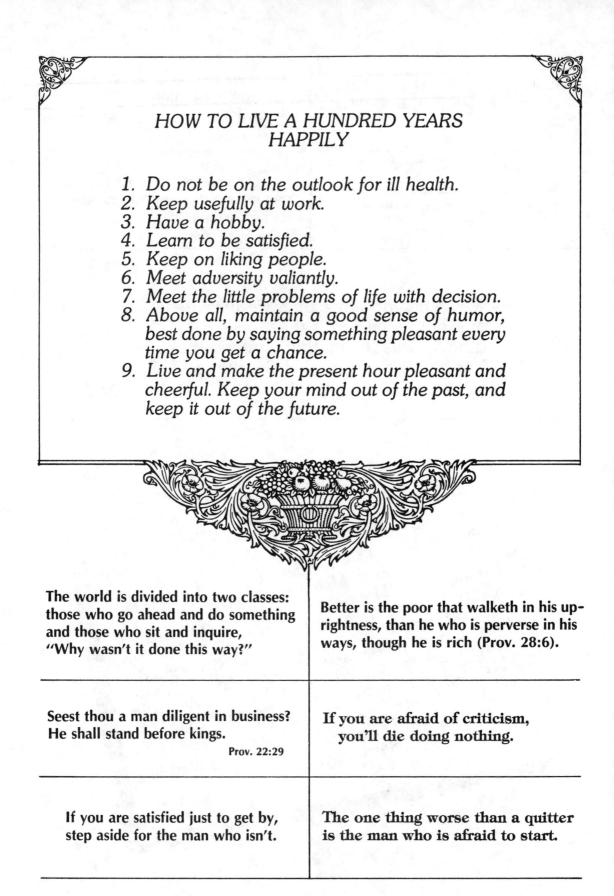

The world is divided into two classes: those who go ahead and do something and those who sit and inquire, "Why wasn't it done this way?"

Better is the poor that walketh in his uprightness, than he who is perverse in his ways, though he is rich (Prov. 28:6).

Seest thou a man diligent in business? He shall stand before kings.

Prov. 22:29

If you are afraid of criticism, you'll die doing nothing.

If you are satisfied just to get by, step aside for the man who isn't.

The one thing worse than a quitter is the man who is afraid to start.

It's the person who has never done anything
who is sure nothing can be done.

There are three ingredients in a good life:
Learning, earning, and yearning.

Where one goes hereafter depends largely
on what one goes after here.

If a man does only what is required of him,
he is a slave.
If a man does more than is required of him,
he is a free man.
—Chinese Proverb

Work is the yeast that raises the dough.

Seest thou a man diligent in business?
He shall stand before kings (Prov. 22:29).

Common sense is seeing things as they are,
and doing things as they should be done.

God desires us to soar like eagles,
but many are content to scratch like sparrows.

Think that day lost whose low descending sun
views from thy hands no noble actions done.
—Bohart

When things seem difficult, and life uphill,
 Don't look too far ahead, keep plodding on,
And inch by inch, the road will shorten, till
 The roughest patches will be past and gone,
And you'll look back surprised and cheered to find
 That you have left so many miles behind,
And very soon the tedious climb will stop,
 And you will stand triumphant at the top.

It is a great thing to do little things well.

Spin CAREFULLY,
Not TEARFULLY,
Though WEARILY you plod.
Spin CAREFULLY,
Spin PRAYERFULLY,
But leave the thread with God.

A TRUE MINISTER
God's man in
God's place, doing
God's work, in
God's way, for
God's glory.

A smooth sea never made a skillful sailor.

Life is like a grindstone, and whether it grinds a man down or polishes him depends on the stuff he is made of.

Poverty is usually the copartner of laziness.

Our responsibility is—
RESPONSE to HIS ABILITY.

Some people have plenty of jawbone but not enough backbone.

A revolving fan gathers no flies.

Let your aim and aspiration be not to enjoy life, but to employ it.

Little strokes fell great oaks.

What you can do,
you ought to do,
and what you
ought to do,
by the help of God
DO!

The dictionary is the only place where you will find SUCCESS before WORK.

Success is 10 percent inspiration and 90 percent perspiration.

The greatest
ABILITY
is
DEPENDABILITY

What is gotten without effort is not worth what it cost.

CONSIDER THE HAMMER

It keeps its head.
It doesn't fly off the handle.
It keeps pounding away.
It finds the point and then drives it home.
It looks at the other side, and thus often
*   clinches the matter.*
It is the only knocker in the world that does any good.

Remember that AMERICAN ends with I CAN.

One way to get ahead
and stay ahead
is to use your head.

Better to try something and fail, than to try nothing and succeed.

Do your duty, that is best;
leave unto the Lord the rest.

Providence sends food for the birds but does not throw it in the nest.

The way to get anywhere is to
start from where you are.

LADDER OF ACHIEVEMENT

100%—I did
90%—I will
80%—I can
70%—I think I can
60%—I might
50%—I think I might
40%—What is it?
30%—I wish I could
20%—I don't know how
10%—I can't
0%—I won't

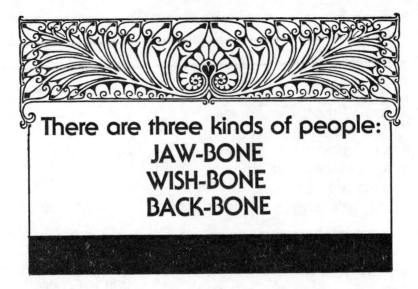

There are three kinds of people:
JAW-BONE
WISH-BONE
BACK-BONE

There are two kinds of men who never amount to much—
those who cannot do what they are told,
and those who can do nothing else.

Even a mosquito doesn't get a slap on the back
until he starts working!

REMEMBER
Every job is a self portrait of
the person who did it.
Autograph your work with excellence.

A good angle to approach any problem is
the TRY-angle.

If it were easy,
anybody could do it.

Do your best and rejoice with him who can do better.

God never calls an idle man.

Nothing is easy to the unwilling.

We never test the resources of God
until we attempt the impossible.

— F. B. Meyer

2/3 of PROMOTION
is MOTION

Success comes in
CANS
Failure comes in
CAN'TS

It is better to fill a little place right
than a big place wrong.

It is not the whistling
that makes a locomotive go,
it is the silent steam.

Life is like a ladder,
every step we take is either
up or down.

Millions of American workers
live in a
CLOCK-EYED WORLD.

Many a man wishes he was as smart as his wife thinks he is.

THE BUSY MAN

If you want to get a favor done
   By some obliging friend,
And want a promise, safe and sure,
   On which you may depend,
Don't go to him who always has
   Much leisure time to plan;
But if you want your favor done,
   Just ask the busy man.
The man with leisure never has
   A moment he can spare,
He's always "putting off" until
   His friends are in despair.
But he whose every waking hour
   Is crowded full of work,
Forgets the art of wasting time,
   He cannot stop to shirk.
So when you want a favor done
   And want it right away,
Go to the man who constantly
   Works twenty hours a day.
He'll find a moment sure, somewhere,
   That has no other use,
And fix you while the idle man
   Is framing an excuse.

My grandfather once told me that there
are two kinds of people; those who do
the work and those who take the credit.
He told me to try to be in the first group;
there was much less competition there.

ANXIETY

It is Thy will that I should cast my every care on Thee;
To Thee refer each rising grief, each new perplexity.
Why should my heart then be distressed by dread of future ill?
Or why should unbelieving fear my trembling spirit fill?

No affliction would trouble the child of God if he knew God's reason for sending it.	The beginning of anxiety is the end of faith, and the beginning of true faith is the end of anxiety.
Those who truly fear God need not fear death.	I know not the way He leads me, but well do I know my Guide. —Martin Luther

Have not one single care,
   One is too much for thee.
The work is Mine and Mine alone,
   Thine is to trust Me.
	If you brood over your troubles, you will have a perfect hatch.

Why, O my soul, those anxious cares?
Why thus cast down with doubts and fears?
How canst thou want if God provide,
Or lose thy way with such a Guide?
He who has helped me hitherto
Will help me all the journey through,
And give me cause to raise
New Ebenezers to His praise.
—J. Newton

When we see the lilies
Spinning in distress,
Taking thought to manufacture
Their own loveliness,
When we see the birds
All building barns for store,
'Twill then be time to worry—
Not before!

NO ANXIOUS CARE
Philippians 4:6

"Be anxious for nothing. . . . "
How could my heart be anxious?
How could my mind be aught but calm and
bold?
When He who keeps the universe in motion
Within His hand my little life doth hold?
If He can hang the earth in space,
And guide its orbit,
If He can make the winds,
And halt their play,
Full well I know He'll keep my soul from faltering,
And guide it surely in His chosen way.

FEAR
is unbelief
parading in disguise

DON'T WORRY
IT MAY NOT HAPPEN!

In every dark, distressing hour,
When sin and Satan join their power,
Let this blest truth repel each dart
That Thou dost bear us on Thy heart.

ATTITUDE

It's a funny thing but true,
The folks you don't like, don't like you.
I don't know why this should be so
But just the same I always know,
That when I'm sour, friends are few,
When I'm friendly, folks are too.
I sometimes get up in the morn,
Awishin' I was never born,
And then I make cross remarks, a few,
And then my family wishes, too,
That I had gone some other place,
But then I change my little tune,
And sing and smile,
And then the folks around me sing and smile.
I guess it was catching all the while.
It's a funny thing but true,
The folks you like, sure like you.

People who never do any more than they get paid for, never get paid for any more than they do.	When an optimist gets the worst of it, he makes the best of it.
When a man is wrong and won't admit it, he always gets angry.	No one can possibly go forward in the strength of the Lord until he has first learned to stand still in his own helplessness.
Many seem determined not to be content with their lot until it is a lot more.	How rare it is to find a person quiet enough to hear God speak.
Nothing gives a person so much advantage over another as to remain cool and unruffled under all circumstances.	A righteous man regardeth the life of his beast; but the tender mercies of the wicked are cruel (Prov. 12:10).

PREJUDICE
is being down on
what we are not
up on.

===

A GRUDGE
is too heavy a load
for anyone
to carry.

===

MELANCHOLY
is the pleasure
of being sad.

===

TROUBLE
is like an
ugly dog—
looks worse coming
than going.

ARE YOU WILLING?

To close the book of complaints and to open the book of praise?

To believe other men are quite as sincere as you are and to treat them with respect?

To ignore what life owes you and to think about what you owe life?

To stop looking for friendship and to start being friendly?

To be content with such things as you have and to stop whining for the things you have not?

To enjoy the simpler blessings and to cease striving for the artificial pleasures of the day?

To forget what you have accomplished and to meditate on what others have done for you?

To cease looking for someone to help you and to devote yourself to helping others?

To accept Jesus Christ as your Savior and to let your life be an outlet for His love, joy and peace?

— The Guide to Light

The PESSIMIST says, "It can't be done."
The OPTIMIST says, "It can be done."
The PEPTIMIST says, "I just did it."

It is easy to major our attention on minor matters.	Let us be less concerned what men think we are than what God knows we are.
A soft answer turneth away wrath; but grievous words stir up anger (Prov. 15:1).	The most important ingredient in the formula of success is knowing how to get along with people.
Nothing will cook your goose faster than a red hot temper.	He who has the most trouble usually has been busy making it.

Forget each kindness that you do as soon as you have done it.
Forget the praise that falls to you the moment you have won it.
Forget the slander that you hear before you can repeat it.
Forget each slight, each spite, each sneer, whenever you may meet it.
Remember every promise made and keep it to the letter.
Remember those who lend you aid and be a grateful debtor.
Remember all the happiness that comes your way in living.
Forget each worry and distress, be hopeful and forgiving.
Remember good, remember truth, remember heaven is above you.
And you will find, through age and youth, that many will love you.

MR. MOODY SAID:
It does not take long to tell where a man's treasure is. In fifteen minutes' conversation with most men, you can tell whether their treasures are on earth or in heaven.

To live above with saints
we love,
O that will be glory!
To live below with saints
we know,
That's a different story.

COMMUNION

1 LET the words of my mouth, and the meditation of my heart, be acceptable in thy sight (Ps. 19:14).

SPEECH

2 LET no corrupt communication proceed out of your mouth (Eph. 4:29).

AFFECTION

3 LET brotherly love continue (Heb. 13:1).

MEDITATION

4 LET the word of Christ dwell in you richly (Col. 3:16).

HUMILITY

5 LET this mind be in you, which was also in Christ Jesus (Phil. 2:5).

QUIETNESS

6 LET the peace of God rule in your hearts (Col. 3:15).

TESTIMONY

7 LET your light so shine before men (Matt. 5:16).

Then let us, brethren, while on earth, with foes
    and strangers mixed,
Be mindful of our heavenly birth, our thoughts
    on glory fixed;
That we should glorify Him here, our Father's
    purpose is:
Whene'er the Savior shall appear, He'll fully
    own us His.

—Choice Gleanings

Apply thyself wholly to the Scriptures and the Scriptures wholly to thyself.

It is a great responsibility to own a Bible.

WHEN YOU READ THE BIBLE THROUGH

I supposed I knew my Bible,
    Reading piecemeal, hit or miss,
Now a bit of John or Matthew,
    Now a snatch of Genesis,
Certain chapter of Isaiah,
    Certain Psalms (the twenty-third),
Twelfth of Romans, First of Proverbs—
    Yes, I thought I knew the Word!
But I found that thorough reading
    Was a different thing to do,
And the way was unfamiliar
    When I read the Bible through.
You who like to play at Bible,
    Dip and dabble, here and there,
Just before you kneel, aweary,
    And yawn through a hurried prayer;
You who treat the Crown of Writings
    As you treat no other book—
Just a paragraph disjointed,
    Just a crude impatient look—
Try a worthier procedure,
    Try a broad and steady view;
You will kneel in very rapture
    When you read the Bible through.

—Amos R. Wells

Some Sure Things

1 Thou shalt surely die. Gen. 2:17.
2 Be sure your sin will find you out. Num. 32:23.
3 The foundation of God standeth sure. II Tim. 2:19.
4 The sure word of prophecy. II Peter 1:19.
5 A hope both sure and steadfast. Heb. 6:19.
6 Surely I come quickly. Rev. 22:20.

—J.C.P.

Books of the Bible
OLD TESTAMENT

In Genesis all things began
That have to do with God and man.

In Exodus the Law was given
To keep our life in tune with heaven.

Leviticus reveals the blood
That kills our sin in crimson flood.

The Book of Numbers shows the way,
How we should walk, and war, and pray.

Deuteronomy, the truth twice told,
It's always fresh and never old.

In Joshua the walls are down,
And Israel's found on Canaan's ground.

In Judges sin doth men enthral,
And yet the Spirit conquers all.

In Ruth the kinsman acts in grace,
To give the gentile bride a place.

In Samuel One is seen King Saul,
His rise and sin and loss and fall.

In Samuel Two King David reigns,
And yet by sin his life he stains.

In First of Kings the Temple's built,
We also read of Israel's guilt.

And Second Kings records the lives
Of prophets, kings, their sons and wives.

In First of Chronicles we're shown
The house of David and his throne.

And Second Chronicles records
The many acts of kings and lords.

In Ezra's journey, work, and prayer,
The traits of grace are everywhere.

Next Nehemiah, who built the wall,
In spite of foes who planned his fall.

The story rich of Esther's tact
Reveals how she with God did act.

In Job, a saint is sorely tried,
And yet by trial is sanctified.

The Psalms are many, good and rare,
They tell of God's unceasing care.

The Proverbs true, with maxims right,
An armor is to fight the fight.

Ecclesiastes—Wisdom's lay,
So never from its precepts stray.

The Song of Songs, it speaks of love,
The Bridegroom fair, the Lord above.

Isaiah's message tells of Him,
Who died to save us from our sin.

In Jeremiah we hear the voice,
As God rebukes the people's choice.

We next behold the prophet weep
In Lamentations strong and deep.

Ezekiel shows us mystic wheels;
And Israel's future, too, reveals.

In Daniel visions we behold;
The reign of Christ is also told.

Hosea sings in holy lays
Of God in all His grace and ways.

In Book of Joel war is rife,
And might of God to still the strife.

In Amos, Judah's raised again,
And in the land with Christ shall reign.

In Obadiah, Jacob's named,
And Edom for his sin is blamed.

In Jonah's freedom from the whale,
We have salvation's wondrous tale.

The Prophet Micah doth relate
The loving God in mercy great.

In Nahum's book a stronghold's found,
That keeps the saint both safe and sound.

In Habakkuk a prayer we hear,
Which bids us worship God and fear.

In Zephaniah, Jehovah sings,
And to the land His people brings.

In Haggai, the Temple's waste;
He bids the people build with haste.

In Zechariah, we visions see,
Of things that are, and those to be.

In Malachi the Lord's the same,
He calls us each to own His claim.

NEW TESTAMENT

In Matthew's theme of Christ the King,
The laws of right with vigor ring.

As Servant true in Mark He's shown,
His acts of service fully known.

The Man of men in Luke behold;
His words and works are clearly told.

In John, as Lord we see His grace;
His truth in all His acts we trace.

In Acts, the Spirit came in might,
To bless His saints and keep them right.

In Romans, next, we're justified;
In Christ we're free and sanctified.

In Corinth I, we read of Love—
The Love so pure, and from above,

In Corinth II, the note resounds,
The grace of God for each abounds.

Galatian saints were wanting sore,
When they would add to grace's score.

Ephesians is a wondrous book;
You'll find all riches if you look.

Colossians tells us "Christ is all."
If we have Him we cannot fall.

Philippians sounds with joy's accord;
We find the joy is in the Lord.

In Thessalonians I we hear
That Christ will come, and soon be here.

In Thessalonians II we see
The man of sin that is to be.

I Timothy—apostle's charge,
To Gospel's word and duties large.

II Timothy to us unfolds
The works of God in all its molds.

In Titus, we have much to learn,
Of grace and glory in their turn.

Philemon is a story sweet,
Where Paul, and slave, and master meet.

In Hebrews, better things we find,
And all in Christ the Priest divined.

In James, we ponder faith that works;
For faith from duty never shirks.

In Peter I, the precious blood
Redeems from sin, and brings to God.

In Peter II to faith we add
The virtue true which maketh glad.

In John the First, in Christ we bide,
And in love of God reside.

In Letter II, the truth, we're told,
Will keep us true with mighty hold.

In John the Third, the apostle's glad,
And also speaks of one that's sad.

In Jude, we read of darkest night,
And faith, and love, and glorious light.

And last, in Revelation grand,
We see the Lamb in glory stand.

There is not an arrow in the quiver of the devil
but has been fired at the Bible and has failed.

The mirror of the Word is painfully clear.	There are multitudes whose Bibles are read (red) only on the edges.
A lot of Christians are living on crackers and cheese when God has prepared three square meals a day for them.	**The degree of our spiritual vigor will be in direct proportion to the time we spend in God's Word.**
The Bible promises no loaves for the loafer.	No atheist can injure the Bible's influence so thoroughly as a Christian who disregards it in his daily life.
The man who samples the Word of God occasionally never acquires much of a taste for it.	**The Bible may cause you to wonder, but it will never cause you to wander.**
We must feed on the Bread of Life ourselves before we can serve it to others.	No man is truly educated who lacks in the knowledge of the Bible.
You can learn a lot from the Bible; you can learn still more practicing it.	**Human supposition can never take the place of divine revelation.**
The Bible will not be a dry book if you know the Author.	The future is as bright as the promises of God.
Look to other books for INFORMATION But look only to the Bible for TRANSFORMATION	**There are two parts to the Gospel: BELIEVING IT and BEHAVING IT.**

Thy testimonies are wonderful: therefore doth my soul keep them. Psalm 119:129

There is a unique harmony in the Bible. In Genesis the earth is created; in Revelation it passes away. In Genesis the sun and moon appear; in Revelation there is no need for the sun or moon. In Genesis there is a garden; the home of man; in Revelation there is a city, the home of the nations. In Genesis we are introduced to Satan; in Revelation we see his doom. In Genesis we hear the first sob and see the first tear; in Revelation we read: "God shall wipe away all tears from their eyes; and there shall be no more death, neither sorrow, nor crying." In Genesis the curse is pronounced; in Revelation we read, "There shall be no more curse." In Genesis we see our first parents driven from the tree of life; in Revelation welcomed back.

Father of mercies in Thy word what endless glory shines!
Forever by Thy name adored for these celestial lines.
Oh, may these heavenly pages be our ever fresh delight;
And still new beauties may we see, and still increasing light.

—A.S.

WHAT GOD HAS DONE WITH OUR SINS

Forgiven and covered them . . . . Psalm 32:1
Not imputed them unto us . . . . . . Psalm 32:2
Removed them . . . . Psalm 103:12
Made them white . . . . Isaiah 1:18
Blotted them out . . . . Isaiah 43:25
Pardoned them . . . . Isaiah 55:7
Cast them into the sea . . . . Micah 7:19
Remitted them . . . . Matthew 26:28
Took them away . . . . John 1:29
Purged them . . . . Hebrews 1:3
Cleansed us from them . . . . I John 1:9
Cast them behind His back . . . . Isaiah 38:17

Study the Bible to be wise; believe it to be safe; practice it to be holy.	When the Word of God is as sweet as honey, the vanities of the world will be bitter as aloes.
No daily meal is complete without the ''Bread of Life.''	Either the Bible will keep you from sin or sin will keep you from the Bible.
Many Christians spend more time reading the newspaper than they do the Bible.	In every step, in every stride, I'll let the Savior be my guide! His Word, His love, I will embrace, And let His wisdom set the pace.

Whatsoever things were written aforetime were written . . . that we through patience and comfort of the scriptures might have hope.
Rom. 15:4.

David said, There is none like that; give it me. I Sam. 21:9.

The Bible is always light-giving in every circumstance of life. "There is none like it." Dr. J. Wilbur Chapman has said, "There's none like it when your head is aching! There's none like it when the day is without the sun and the night without its star. There is nothing like it when your children are motherless! There is none like it when you bury your baby! There's none like it when the springs of life are snapping! There is none like it when you reach the end of life's journey and pillow your head on its promises and God stoops and kisses you to sleep."

This Book of God I'd rather own than all the gold and gems

That are in monarch's coffers shone, than all their diadems.

— Choice Gleanings

BIBLE BE'S

"Be ye therefore perfect." Matt. 5:48

"Be patient." James 5:7

"Be at peace." Job 22:21

"Be of good cheer; it is I; be not afraid." Matt. 14:27

"Be diligent that ye may be found of Him in peace, without spot and blameless." II Peter 3:14

"Be subject one to another." I Peter 5:5

"Be clothed with humility." I Peter 5:8

"Be sober, be vigilant." I Peter 5:8

"Be ye kind one to another, tenderhearted, forgiving one another." Eph. 4:32

"Be strong and of good courage." Josh. 1:6

The people of Nineveh believed God.
Jonah 3:5

This is one of the most remarkable statements in the story. But it never seems to make the impression the whale does. The swallowing of a little man by a big fish is merely a matter of size. The man has only to be small enough and the fish big enough and the job is done. But for that little prophet to walk into New York, Chicago, Philadelphia, London, or any other city and bring that city to repentance and belief in God is some achievement! Why doesn't the professor get funny about that — which is really the point of the story.

God . . . . .The greatest Lover
So loved . . . . .The greatest Degree
The world . . . . .The greatest Company
That He gave . . . . .The greatest Act
HIS only begotten SON . . . . .The greatest Gift
That whosoever . . . .The greatest Opportunity
Believeth . . . . .The greatest Simplicity
In HIM . . . . .The greatest Attraction
Should not perish . . . . . . .The greatest Promise
But . . . . .The greatest Difference
Have . . . . .The greatest Certainty
Eternal Life . . . . .The greatest Possession
John 3:16

We may tremble ON the Rock of Ages,
but the Rock will never tremble
UNDER us.

The only objection against the Bible is a bad life.

Man could not have written the Bible if he would,
and would not if he could.

THE TEN COMMANDMENTS IN RHYME
1 Thou no gods shalt have but Me.
2 Before no idol bow the knee.
3 Take not the name of God in vain.
4 Dare not the Sabbath Day profane.
5 Give to thy parents honor due.
6 Take heed that thou no murder do.
7 Abstain from words and deeds unclean.
8 Steal not, for thou by God art seen.
9 Tell no willful lie and love it.
10 What is thy neighbor's do not covet.

The Bible
(Heb. 4:12, 13; II Tim. 3:15, 16)

THIS BOOK contains the mind of God, the state of man, the way of salvation, the doom of sinners, and the happiness of believers. Its doctrines are holy, its precepts are binding, its histories are true, and its decisions are immutable.

READ IT TO BE WISE, believe it to be safe, and practise it to be holy. It contains light to direct you, food to support you, and comfort to cheer you. It is the traveler's map, the pilgrim's staff, the pilot's compass, the soldier's sword, and the Christian's charter. Here Paradise is restored, Heaven opened, and the gates of hell disclosed.

CHRIST IS ITS GRAND SUBJECT, our good its design, and the glory of God its end. It should fill the memory, rule the heart, and guide the feet.

READ IT SLOWLY, frequently, prayerfully. It is a mine of wealth, a paradise of glory, and a river of pleasure. It is given you in life, will be opened at the judgment, and be remembered for ever. It involves the highest responsibility, will reward the greatest labor, and condemns all who trifle with its sacred contents.

—PRISCILLA HOWE

THE WORD OF GOD

For feelings come and feelings go,
And feelings are deceiving;
My warrant is the Word of God
Nought else is worth believing.
I'll trust in God's unchanging Word
Till soul and body sever:
For, though all things shall pass away,
His Word shall stand forever.

A knowledge of the Bible without a college education is more valuable than a college education without a knowledge of the Bible.

How rare it is to find a person quiet enough to hear God speak.

Beneath me green pastures, beside me still waters,
   And with me my Shepherd to lead every day.
Before me a table, and enemies round me;
   Behind goodness, mercy—o'ershadow my way.
Beyond me the house of the Lord ever loometh;
   And soon I'll be home with my Shepherd for aye.

Our Bible contains 810,697 words. This is about four times as many as are found in a book of average length. Although so long a book and dealing with the greatest theme that can engage the mind of man, its vocabulary is singularly limited. Only 6,000 different words are used; which is very small compared to the 20,000 employed by Shakespeare in writing his plays. Not only is the vocabulary limited, but the average word in the Bible contains but five letters. Many of these short words in the Bible are, however, full of the deepest meaning and are worthy of earnest study. Such as these short five-letter words, grace, peace, faith, saved, serve, glory, and Jesus.

—from Oxford University Press

When the Bible speaks discussion is useless; when the Bible is silent discussion ends.

When you study the Scriptures "hit and miss," you miss more than you hit.

THOMAS JEFFERSON SAID

The studious perusal of the Sacred Volume will make better citizens, better fathers, and better husbands.

But fixed from everlasting years,
Unmoved amidst the wrecks of spheres,
Thy Word shall shine in cloudless day,
When heaven and earth have passed away.

The best thing to do with the Bible is to
know it in the head,
stow it in the heart,
sow it in the world,
and show it in the life.

BRIEF RULES FOR BIBLE STUDY

1 **Read it through (get something definite).**
2 **Pray it in (apply it).**
3 **Write it down (mark your Bible).**
4 **Work it out (in daily life).**
5 **Pass it on (tell others).**

YOUR OWN VERSION

You are writing a Gospel,
A chapter each day,
By deeds that you do,
By words that you say.
Men read what you write,
Whether faithless or true;
Say, what is the Gospel
According to YOU?

— Gilbert

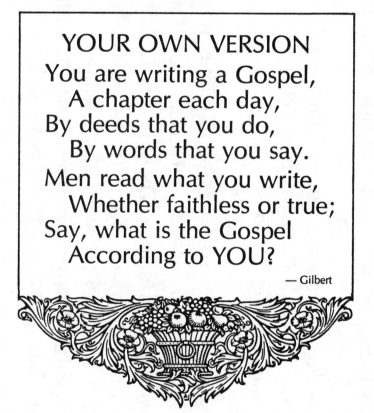

The NEW is in the OLD contained;
The OLD is in the NEW explained;
The NEW is in the OLD concealed;
The OLD is in the NEW revealed.

THE SEVEN WONDERS OF THE BIBLE

There are the seven wonders of the world. But here are seven wonders of the Word.

1 The wonder of its formation, i.e., the mysterious method of its formation. The way in which the Bible grew is one of the mysteries of time.

2 The wonder of its unification. It is a library of sixty-six books, yet one Book.

3 The wonder of its age. It is the most ancient of all books.

4 The wonder of its sale. It is the bestseller of any book.

5 The wonder of its interest. The only book in the world read by all classes.

6 The wonder of its language. Although written largely by uneducated men, it is the best from a literary standpoint.

7 The wonder of its preservation. It has been the most hated book of all books. Time and again efforts have been made to annihilate it, yet it still exists.

"The word of our God shall stand for ever."

— HiCal

Should I do it? Should I say it? Should I think it? Answer me!
Should I hear . . . or write . . . or read it? Should I go . . . or should I see?
So the endless "Or's" or "Why nots" seek an answer to their probe;
Yet, God's Word is all-sufficient filmsy reasonings to disrobe.

M.C.

Despond then no longer;
The Lord will provide;
And this be the token—
No Word He hath spoken
Hath ever been broken;
THE LORD WILL PROVIDE.

PREACHER, PREACH THE WORD!

Give them this LAMP to light the road;
This STOREHOUSE for their daily food;
Give them this CHART for life's rough sea;
This BALM to sooth their wounds;
Yes, preacher, PREACH THE WORD!

There are three means of assurance of salvation. They may be called external, internal, and evidential.
EXTERNAL is assurance by the Word of God,
INTERNAL is by the witness of the Spirit,
EVIDENTIAL is by the fruit in the life.

THE FRUIT OF THE SPIRIT—LOVE

JOY is love exulting.
PEACE is love in repose.
LONGSUFFERING is love on trial.
GENTLENESS is love in society.
GOODNESS is love in action.
FAITH is love in endurance.
MEEKNESS is love at school.
TEMPERANCE is love in discipline.

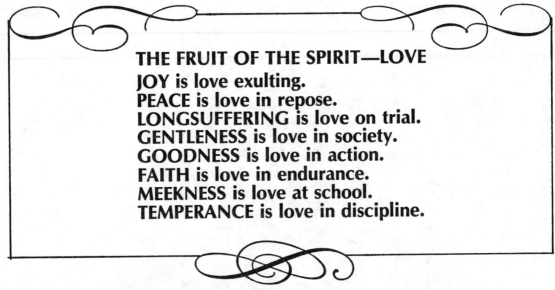

If it is in the Bible, it is SO!

Each word is like a gem,
From the celestial mines,
A sunbeam from that holy heaven
Where holy sunlight shines.

— H. Bonar

MEDICINE CHEST

For the BLUES ....read Ps. 27.
For an EMPTY PURSE ....read Ps. 37.
If DISCOURAGED about work ..read Ps. 128.
If people seem UNKIND to you .read John 15.
If you are losing CONFIDENCE
    in people ....read I Cor. 13.
If you cannot have YOUR OWN
    WAY ....read James 3.
If you are all OUT OF SORTS ..read Heb. 12.
For a TRAVELING COMPANION read Ps. 121.

BLESSINGS

I recognize the sublime truth announced in the Holy Scriptures and proven by all history that those nations only are blessed whose God is the Lord.

—Abraham Lincoln

His way is best,
I cease from needless scheming
and leave the ruling
of my life to Him.
All will be well,
though now all wrong, 'tis seeming.
All will be clear
that now to me seems dim.
So I am blest.

No matter how great our need,
the divine resources are never exhausted.

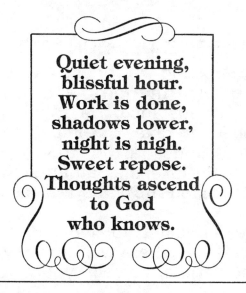

Quiet evening,
blissful hour.
Work is done,
shadows lower,
night is nigh.
Sweet repose.
Thoughts ascend
to God
who knows.

Clouds in our lives
are sent many times
to bring showers of blessings.

THE CROWD AND GOD
The atheist shouted.
"Down with God!" he said,
And all the thousands shouted too.
Fourteen thousand in an armory,
And all shouted—
Shouted against God!
I read it in the paper one morning
As I took the Boston plane;
And as I read it,
Down below was the armory,
The mob of threateners now gone.
Three thousand feet down
The armory looked so small.
And the shouts would not have been heard
Had they been shouting and threatening me.
Then I read the Second Psalm
And saw God smiling in derision.

Will Houghton

WHERE JESUS FOUND THEM—

It's interesting to notice where Jesus found some of the folks who became His friends. For instance, He found Matthew busy collecting taxes in the customshouse, Nathanael under a fig tree, Peter and Andrew at the lake, the Samaritan woman at a well, Zacchaeus up a tree, and the thief on a cross.

Where did He find you when He called you to follow Him? Where will He find you when He comes again, or calls you to come up higher?

—Roy J. Wilkins

What fruit have ye from the things whereof ye are now ashamed? For the end of those things is death (Rom. 6:21)

A man has to live with himself, and he should see to it that he always has good company.

If you were another person, would you like to be a friend of yourself?

The world is the better or the worse for everyone who lives in it.

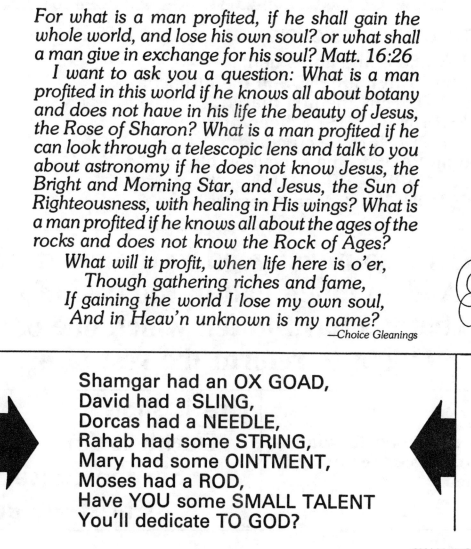

For what is a man profited, if he shall gain the whole world, and lose his own soul? or what shall a man give in exchange for his soul? Matt. 16:26

I want to ask you a question: What is a man profited in this world if he knows all about botany and does not have in his life the beauty of Jesus, the Rose of Sharon? What is a man profited if he can look through a telescopic lens and talk to you about astronomy if he does not know Jesus, the Bright and Morning Star, and Jesus, the Sun of Righteousness, with healing in His wings? What is a man profited if he knows all about the ages of the rocks and does not know the Rock of Ages?

What will it profit, when life here is o'er,
Though gathering riches and fame,
If gaining the world I lose my own soul,
And in Heav'n unknown is my name?
—Choice Gleanings

Shamgar had an OX GOAD,
David had a SLING,
Dorcas had a NEEDLE,
Rahab had some STRING,
Mary had some OINTMENT,
Moses had a ROD,
Have YOU some SMALL TALENT
You'll dedicate TO GOD?

AS A GOOD SOLDIER OF JESUS CHRIST.
IITim. 2:3
I HAVE FOUGHT A GOOD FIGHT. IITim. 4:7

You are enlisted, you wear the uniform, you ought to fight; victory is certain, the honors are everlasting — think only of Him who is your "Leader and Commander." You will have no such opportunity of distinguishing yourselves for Christ in heaven. Lose no time, then, in waking up to the consciousness that you are soldiers, and that you must learn to fight. There is no discharge in this war, and no truce with the enemy.

—*Choice Gleanings*

FAITHFULNESS TO CHRIST—

Put DANIEL in the lion's den;
Cast his THREE FRIENDS in the furnace;
Made STEPHEN the first martyr;
Took JOHN BAPTIST'S head off;
Caused PETER to be crucified;
Brought PAUL to the execution block;
Burned EARLY CHRISTIANS at the stake.
QUESTION: What does it cost us?

**There's so much good in the worst of us,
And so much bad in the best of us,
That it's hard to tell which one of us
Ought to reform the rest of us.**

For every benefit you receive, a responsibility is levied.

Life is short
Death is sure
Sin the cause
Christ the cure.

If you want to be DISTRESSED, look within.
If you want to be DEFEATED, look back.
If you want to be DISTRACTED, look around.
If you want to be DISMAYED, look before.
If you want to be DELIVERED, look up.
If you want to be DELIGHTED, look to Christ.

Shoes divide men into three classes.
Some wear their father's shoes, they make no declaration of their own.
Some are unthinkingly shod by the crowd.
The strong man is his own cobbler; he insists on making his own choices. He walks in his own shoes.

—S. D. Gordon

ONLY
One life
'twill soon be past
ONLY
What's done for Christ
Will last!

CHARACTER

The cause, not the pain, makes the martyr.	Fads come and go; common sense goes on forever.
A bad conscience has a good memory.	What you laugh at tells plainer than words what you are.
A beautiful heart seems to transform the homeliest face.	Character is what you are in the dark.
There is nothing truly great in any man—except character.	It is better to be short of cash than to be short of character.
Behavior is a mirror in which we show our image.	Character is not made in a crisis—it is only exhibited.
Manners carry the world for the moment; character for all times.	A golden character needs no gilding.
Character needs no epitaph. You can bury a man, but character will beat the hearse back from the graveyard.	What you possess in this world will go to someone else when you die, but what you are will be yours forever.
Our true selves are usually revealed in our seemingly trivial acts.	The measure of a man's real character is what he would do if he knew he would never be found out.

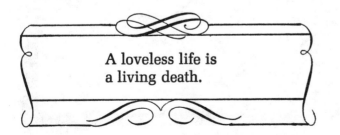

'Tis beauty that doth oft make women proud;
'Tis virtue that doth make them most admired;
'Tis modesty that makes them seem divine.

Your character is what God knows you to be.
Your reputation is what men think you are.

A loveless life is
a living death.

It is HUMAN
to stand with the
CROWD.
It is DIVINE
to stand
ALONE.

CHRIST

The Paradoxes of Christ

He was the Light, yet He hung in darkness on the Cross.

He was the Life, yet He poured out His soul unto death.

He was the Rock of Ages, yet His feet sank into the deep waters.

He was the Son of God, yet He died a felon's death.

He was holy, undefiled, separated from sinners and knew no sin, yet He was "made sin" when He took the guilty culprit's place and suffered in his stead.

He bade the weary to come to Him for rest, yet not on earth could He find rest until He said, "It is finished," and gave up His life to God.

He was the Mighty God, yet He became a man and was crucified through weakness.

He was the Image of the Invisible God, yet His visage was marred more than any man.

All the fulness of the Godhead dwells bodily in Him, yet He took on Him the form of a servant and was made in the likeness of men.

He spake, and it was done; he commanded, and it stood fast; yet He humbled Himself and became obedient — even unto death.

He was the Desire of All Nations, yet He was despised and rejected of man.

He is the Fountain of Life, yet upon the Cross He cried, "I thirst."

Can you understand these mysteries? These are the things that angels desire to look into. The heaven cannot contain Him, yet He died for us.

—Faithful Words

Some time ago a poor weaver in Scotland preached a brief sermon on three texts: (1) "The Blood of Jesus Christ cleanseth from all sin." He said: "That's my sin awa." (2) "Are not five sparrows sold for two farthings, and not one of them is forgotten before God. Ye are of more value than many sparrows." "That's my cares awa." (3) "We shall be caught up to meet the Lord in the air." "And that's myself awa."

If I have Jesus only
I'm safe for eternity.
If I have everything else
Without Him I am lost.

Jesus was content with a stable when he was born that we might have a mansion when we die.	Christ sends none away empty except those who are full of themselves.
Nature FORMS us, Sin DEFORMS us, School INFORMS us, but only Christ TRANSFORMS US.	If Christ is THE WAY, why waste time traveling some OTHER WAY?

Life with Christ is an endless hope; life without Christ is a hopeless end.	Christ is needed on the avenue as much as in the alley.
He that is mastered by Christ is the master of many circumstances.	Holiness is not the way to Christ, Christ is the way to holiness.
If you would master temptation, let Christ master you.	It is better to be with Christ in the storm than in smooth water without Him.
Peace rules the day when Christ rules the soul.	If we want an increase of Christ, there must first be a decrease of self.

CHRIST IS THE WAY— men without Him are like Cain, wanderers and vagabonds.

CHRIST IS THE TRUTH— men without Him are liars, like the devil.

CHRIST IS THE LIGHT— men without Him walk in darkness and know not whither they go.

CHRIST IS THE LIFE— men without Him are dead in trespasses and sin.

CHRIST IS THE VINE— men who are not in Him are withered branches prepared for the fire.

CHRIST IS THE ROCK— men not built on Him are carried away by the flood of judgment.

O BLESSED CHRIST, how much better would it not to be, than to be without Thee!

ISN'T HE WONDERFUL!

For unto us a child is born, unto us a son is given . . . ; and his name shall be called Wonderful. Isa. 9:6

Everything about Christ is remarkable. Of Him it was said, "[He] hath done nothing amiss" (Luke 23:4), "I find no fault in [Him]" (John 7:46), and "Certainly this was a righteous man" (Luke 23:47). God himself declared from Heaven, "This is my beloved Son; hear him" (Mark 9:7). Yes, Jesus is unique and amazing because He is the only One who is both truly divine and sinlessly human.

An unknown author exclaims with wonder and adoration: "Christ came from the bosom of the Father to the bosom of a woman. He put on humanity that we might put on divinity. (See II Peter 1:4.) He became a man that we might become the sons of God. In infancy He startled a king; in boyhood He puzzled the doctors; in manhood He ruled the course of nature. He walked upon the billows, hushed the sea to sleep, and healed the multitudes without medicine. He never wrote a book; yet the libraries of the world are filled with volumes that have been written about Him. He never penned a musical note; yet He is the theme of more lyrics than any other subject in the world. Great men have come and gone; yet He lives on. Herod could not kill Him, Satan could not seduce Him, death could not destroy Him, the grave could not hold Him. All others have failed in some way, but not Jesus! This perfect One is 'altogether lovely.'"

Not only is Christ matchless in His person and accomplishments, He is absolutely thrilling to know as Savior and Friend. With Isaiah and millions of redeemed souls, I can testify that Jesus is truly WONDERFUL!

—H. G. B.
Our Daily Bread

What think ye of Christ . . .
—Matt. 22:42

PILATE, what do you think of this Man?
"I find no fault in Him at all."

JUDAS? "I have sinned in that I have betrayed innocent blood."

CENTURION? "Truly this was the Son of God."

JOHN THE BAPTIST? "The Lamb of God which taketh away . . . sin."

JOHN? "He is the bright and morning star."

PETER? "Thou art the Christ, the Son of the Living God."

THOMAS? "My Lord and my God."

PAUL? "The excellency of the knowledge of Christ Jesus my Lord."

ANGELS IN HEAVEN? "A Savior which is Christ the Lord."

FATHER IN HEAVEN? "My Beloved Son in whom I am well pleased."

"What think ye of Christ" is the test,
To try both your state and your mien,
You cannot be right on the rest,
Unless you think rightly of Him.

Though Christ a thousand times in Bethlehem be born,
if He's not born in thy soul, thy soul is forlorn.

To lose all for Christ is my best gain;
and to gain without Him would be my worst loss.

The cross of Christ reveals man's sin at its worst, but God's love at its best.

NEVER MAN SPAKE LIKE THIS MAN.　　John 7:46.

Before Abraham was, I AM. John 8:58.

I AM the bread of life, John 6:35

I AM the light of the world. John 8:12.

I AM the door. John 10:7.

I AM the good shepherd. John 10:11.

I AM the resurrection, and the life. John 11:25.

I AM the way, the truth, and the life. John 14:6.

I AM the true vine. John 15:1.

Lamb of God! our souls adore Thee while upon Thy face we gaze;
There the Father's love and glory shine in all their brightest rays:
Thy Almighty power and wisdom, all creation's works proclaim;
Heaven and earth alike confess Thee as the ever great I AM.

If ye believe not that I AM he, ye shall die in your sins. John 8:24.

—Choice Gleanings

Jesus who died to save us, now lives to keep us.

Christ is not VALUED AT ALL unless He is valued ABOVE ALL.	Jesus Christ is no security against storms, but He is a perfect security in storms. He has never promised you an easy passage, only a safe landing.

If you want to know how precious Christ can be, make Him pre-eminent.

CENTER your Christmas in CHRIST

The Son of God became the Son of Man
that he might change
the sons of men into sons of God.

**Christ is our Peace; the sins of YESTERDAY
By His most precious blood are washed away.
Christ is our Life; the trials of TODAY
He bears for us who walked life's toilsome way.
Christ is our Hope; the FUTURE all unknown
Is in His care who watches from the throne.**

SOMEONE HAS SAID:

The solution to the American family problems
is contained in one word—CHRIST.

CHRIST at the marriage altar,
CHRIST on the bridal journey,
CHRIST when the new home is set up,
CHRIST when the baby comes,
CHRIST in the pinching times,
CHRIST in the days of plenty,
CHRIST when the wedded pair walk toward
     sunset gates,
CHRIST when one is taken and the other left,
CHRIST in time, CHRIST for eternity.
THIS IS THE SECRET of a happy home life.

CHRISTIAN

VICTORY

When you are forgotten, or neglected, or purposely set at naught, and you smile inwardly, glorying in the oversight
— THAT IS VICTORY.

When your good is evil spoken of, your taste offended, your advice disregarded, your opinion ridiculed, and you take it all in patient and loving silence
— THAT IS VICTORY

When you are content with any food, any raiment, any climate, any interruption
— THAT IS VICTORY.

When you care never to refer to yourself in conversation, or to record your own good work, or to seek after commendation, when you can truly "love to be unknown"
—THAT IS VICTORY.

"If you desire Himself alone to fill you, For Him alone you care to live and be: Then 'tis not you, but Christ who dwelleth in you,
And that, O child of God, is VICTORY."

"But thanks be to God, which giveth us the victory through our Lord, Jesus Christ."

I Cor. 15:57

**The Word is solemn—don't TRIFLE;
The task is difficult—don't RELAX;
The opportunity is brief—don't DELAY;
The path is narrow—don't WANDER;
The prize is glorious—don't FAINT.**

He always wins who sides with God; to Him no cause is lost.

Christians never meet for the last time.

The Christian who claims the promises of God should obey the commands of God.

Reckon him a Christian indeed who is not ashamed of the Gospel nor a shame to it.

If you are a Christian, remember that men judge your Lord by you.

The secret of being a saint is being a saint in secret.

One with God is a majority.

He who is born of God should grow to resemble his father.

A Christian is free but not free to sin.

A Christian is one who does not have to consult his bank book to see how wealthy he really is.

We should be
    a PUZZLE to the outsider,
    a TERROR to the devil,
    a JOY to Him who bought
        us with His precious blood.

*Learn to BEAR
    and to FORBEAR,
        FORGET
        and FORGIVE;
For this is the way all
    Christians should live.*

CHRISTIAN

It is not the ship in the water but the water in the ship that sinks it. So it is not the Christian in the world but the world in the Christian that constitutes the danger.

Anything that dims my vision of Christ, or takes away my taste for Bible study, or cramps my prayer life, or makes Christian work difficult, is wrong for me, and I must, as a Christian, turn away from it.
— J. Wilbur Chapman

IF YOU ARE NOT A CHRISTIAN, WHY NOT?
SEVEN REASONS

1. Is it because you are afraid of ridicule, and of what others may say of you? "Whosoever shall be ashamed of me and my words; of him shall the Son of man be ashamed."

2. Is it because of the inconsistencies of professing Christians? "Every man shall give an account of himself to God."

3. Is it because you are not willing to give up all for Christ? "What shall it profit a man to gain the whole world and lose his own soul?"

4. Is it because you are afraid you will not be accepted? "Him that cometh unto me I will in no wise cast out."

5. Is it because you fear you are too great a sinner? "Though your sins be as scarlet, they shall be as white as snow, though they be red like crimson, they shall be as wool."

6. Is it because you think you are doing the best you can, and God ought to be satisfied with that? "Whosoever shall keep the whole law, and offend in one point is guilty of all."

7. Is it because you think there is time enough yet? "Boast not thyself of tomorrow, for thou knowest not what a day may bring forth."

A SOLEMN QUESTION

If you were arrested
for being a Christian,

Would there be enough evidence
to convict you?

HIS UNSPEAKABLE GIFT.

                              II Cor. 9:15
HEARD UNSPEAKABLE WORDS.

                              II Cor. 12:4
REJOICE WITH JOY UNSPEAKABLE.

                              I Peter 1:8

Unspeakable is only used three times in the New Testament.

Each word translated "unspeakable" is a totally different word in Greek.

1. Thanks be to God for His "indescribable" gift.

2. Caught up into Paradise and heard "unpublished" words.

3. We rejoice with joy "unutterable" and full of glory.

—Lieut. G. Mascull

An old Puritan said,
if you are a child of God
and you marry a child of
the devil,
you will be sure to have
trouble with your
father-in-law.

A living
CHRIST
in a living
MAN
is a living
SERMON.

CHRIST FOR ME

**The PRESENCE of Christ
Is the JOY of my life.
The SERVICE of Christ
Is the BUSINESS of my life.
The WILL of Christ
Is the LAW of my life.
The GLORY of Christ
Is the CROWN of my life.**

CHRISTIAN AFFECTION

"Be KINDLY AFFECTIONED one to another"   Rom. 12:10

"LOVE one another"   Rom. 13:8

"Be LIKEMINDED one toward another"   Rom. 15:5

"RECEIVE ye one another"   Rom. 15:7

"SAME CARE for one another"   I Cor. 12:25

"FORBEARING one another in love"   Eph. 4:2

"FORGIVING one another"Col. 4:2

"COMFORT one another"   I Thess. 4:18

"EDIFY one another" I Thess. 5:11

"CONSIDER one another"   Heb. 10:24

"PRAY for one another" James 5:16

"Use HOSPITALITY one to another"   I Peter 4:9

A CHRISTIAN IS

A MIND—through which Christ THINKS.
A VOICE—through which Christ SPEAKS.
A HEART—through which Christ LOVES.
A HAND—through which Christ HELPS.

Heathen are true to false gods,
while Christians are false to the true God.

**A Christian should aspire to
do the will of God:
nothing MORE,
nothing LESS,
nothing ELSE.**

No man ever regretted
CHRISTIANITY
on his deathbed.

*Men are religious naturally,
but Christians supernaturally.*

*JESUS first,
YOURSELF last,
and NOTHING between
spells
    J O Y
in the true sense.*

*Christians are not sinless,
but they should sin less.*

**In the Christian life we must lose to gain; we must give to obtain; we
must be humble to be exalted; we must be least to be greatest; we
must die to live.**

Real Christians are forgiven, forgiving, and for giving.
Their sins are forgiven by God.
They themselves forgive those who wrong them.
And a generous spirit prompts them to give cheerfully
*   to the work of the Lord.*

— R. L. Cox

FAITH makes a man a Christian.
His LIFE proves he is a Christian.
TRIAL confirms him as a Christian
DEATH crowns him as a Christian.

*Christians are like tea: their strength
is not drawn out until they get in hot
water.*

On the phrase, "IN CHRIST" hinges Paul's Epistles.
ROMANS has to do with being JUSTIFIED in Christ;
EPHESIANS, with being UNITED in Christ;
PHILIPPIANS, with being SATISFIED in Christ;
THESSALONIANS, with being GLORIFIED in Christ.

LIVING CHRISTIANITY

In the home it's KINDNESS

In business it's HONESTY

In society it's COURTESY

In work it's FAITHFULNESS

Toward the unfortunate it's PITY

Toward the weak it's HELP

Toward the wicked it's RESISTANCE

Toward the strong it's TRUST

Toward the penitent it's FORGIVENESS

Toward the fortunate it's CONGRATULATION

Toward God it's OBEDIENCE.

REGENERATION—A change of NATURE; a new life FROM God.
REPENTANCE—A change of MIND; a new mind ABOUT God.
CONVERSION—A change of LIFE; a new life FOR God.
JUSTIFICATION—A change of STATE; a new standing BEFORE God.
SANCTIFICATION—A change of SERVICE; separation UNTO God.
ADOPTION—A change of FAMILY; a new relationship BEFORE God.
GLORIFICATION—A change of PLACE; a new condition WITH God.

What it Costs to be True to God

It cost Abraham the yielding up of his only son.
It cost Daniel to be cast into the den of lions.
It cost Stephen death by stoning.
It cost Peter a martyr's death.
It cost Jesus His life.
DOES IT COST YOU ANYTHING?

If your Christianity is worth having, it should be worth sharing.

Just because a Christian smokes is not a sign that he is on fire for God.

FRUIT OF THE SPIRIT — LOVE
Gal. 5:22, 23

JOY is love in exulting.
PEACE is love in repose.
LONGSUFFERING is love on trial.
GENTLENESS is love in society.
GOODNESS is love in action.
FAITH is love in endurance.
MEEKNESS is love at school.
TEMPERANCE is love in discipline.

Two marks of a Christian:
GIVING
and
FORGIVING

Every Christian must witness, for there is an impelling
GO
in the GOSPEL.

THE CHRISTIAN IN CHRIST

In death TOGETHER . . . . II Tim. 2:11

Made alive TOGETHER . . . . Eph. 2:5

Raised TOGETHER . . . . Eph. 2:6

In heavenly places TOGETHER . . . . Eph. 2:6

Returning TOGETHER . . . . Col. 3:4

Heirs TOGETHER . . . . Rom. 8:17

Reigning TOGETHER . . . . Rev. 20:4

Forever TOGETHER . . . . I Thess. 4:17

He knows His sheep; He counts them, and He
   calleth them by name.
He goes before; they follow as He leads
   through flood or flame.
He leads them out, into the pastures green by
   waters still;
He leads them in; and guards them safe
   within the fold from ill.

—Choice Gleanings

We've been experiencing great enjoyment in practicing "Christian Cancellation." It works like this: A good word cancels a bad word. A truth cancels a lie. A smile cancels a frown. "Praise the Lord!" from you cancels an oath from someone else. A prayer cancels a pain. Contact paper applied to a public washroom wall cancels out obscenities. A word of encouragement to your pastor cancels out discouragement. A gift cancels out debt. You can think of lots more. We're incorporating a ministry to be known as "Christ's Cancelors." Help cancel out the Devil! Let's together make this a great year of "Christian cancellation!"

— Alex Dunlap, Director of The Conversion Center

It is not what we EAT but what we DIGEST that
   makes us STRONG.
Not what we GAIN but what we SAVE that
   makes us RICH.
Not what we READ but what we REMEMBER that
   makes us LEARNED.
Not what we PROFESS but what we PRACTICE that
   makes us CHRISTIANS.

Christian, don't drive your stakes too deep; we're moving in the morning.

Conversion may be the work of a moment, but a saint is not made overnight.

Christianity is PERSONAL (purse-and-all).

Christians can get weary IN their work, but never OF their work.

Some Christians are like the Arctic rivers—frozen at the mouth.

No garment is more becoming to a Christian than the CLOAK of humility.

THE CHRISTIAN LIFE COMPARED TO—
An EAGLE hastening to the prey (Job 9:26)
A PILGRIMAGE (Gen. 47:9)
A TALE told (Ps. 90:9)
A SWIFT POST (Job 9:25)
A SWIFT SHIP (Job 9:26)
A HAND-BREATH (Ps. 39:5)
A SHEPHERD'S TENT removed (Isa. 38:8)
A DREAM (Ps. 73:20)
A SLEEP (Ps. 90:5)
A VAPOR (James 4:14)
A SHADOW (Eccles. 6:12)
A THREAD cut by the weaver (Isa. 38:12)
A WEAVER'S SHUTTLE (Job 7:6)
A FLOWER (Job 14:2)
GRASS (I Peter 1:24)
WATER spilled on the ground (II Sam. 14:14)
WIND (Job 7:7)

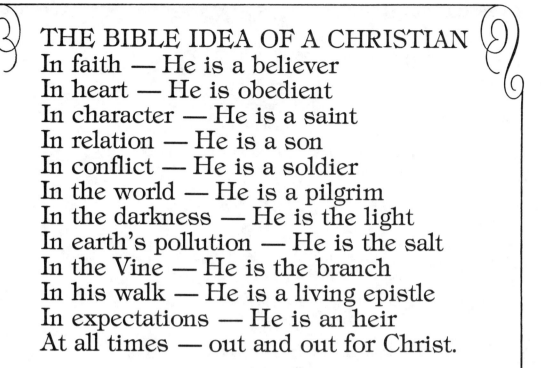

THE BIBLE IDEA OF A CHRISTIAN
In faith — He is a believer
In heart — He is obedient
In character — He is a saint
In relation — He is a son
In conflict — He is a soldier
In the world — He is a pilgrim
In the darkness — He is the light
In earth's pollution — He is the salt
In the Vine — He is the branch
In his walk — He is a living epistle
In expectations — He is an heir
At all times — out and out for Christ.

DEATH—WHAT IS IT?
We think of death as ENDING,
For the Christian it is a glorious BEGINNING;
We think of it as GOING AWAY;
But it is really a wondrous ARRIVING!

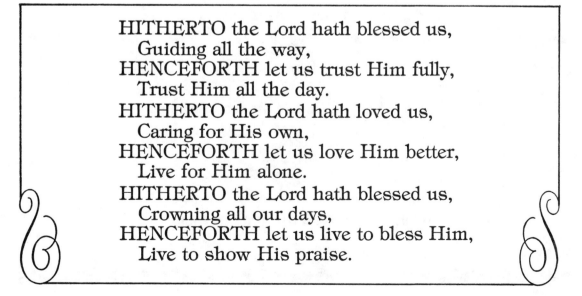

HITHERTO the Lord hath blessed us,
   Guiding all the way,
HENCEFORTH let us trust Him fully,
   Trust Him all the day.
HITHERTO the Lord hath loved us,
   Caring for His own,
HENCEFORTH let us love Him better,
   Live for Him alone.
HITHERTO the Lord hath blessed us,
   Crowning all our days,
HENCEFORTH let us live to bless Him,
   Live to show His praise.

A stranger is one away from home,
but a pilgrim is one who is on his way home.

It is wonderful to be on the "ins" with God
and on the "outs" with nobody but the devil.
—T. J. Bach

Reckon him a Christian indeed who is not ashamed of
the Gospel nor a shame to it.

Only those who are truly BOUND to Christ
are truly FREE.

It costs nothing to become a Christian,
but it costs everything to be a Christian.

Christians, like pianos, need frequent tuning.

The Christian's life is the world's Bible.

Nothing can make a trusting Christian blue.

What we need in these hectic days is a Christian CALMplex.

Every true Christian can boast
of having three degrees;
    B.A. — Born Again
    M.A. — Mightily Altered
    D.D. — Divinely Destined.

Day by day,
dear Lord,
of Thee three things I pray:
    to see Thee more clearly,
      to love Thee more dearly,
        and to follow Thee more truly
day by day.

Scripture gives four names to Christians:
    SAINTS for their holiness,
    BELIEVERS for their faith,
    BRETHREN for their love,
    DISCIPLES for their knowledge.

To return evil for good is DEVILISH:
To return good for good is HUMAN;
To return good for evil is GOD-LIKE.

Five things are seen in connection with the sheep:
(1) The Believer's Relationship - "My sheep."
(2) The Believer's Privilege - "Hear My voice."
(3) The Believer's Walk - "Follow Me."
(4) The Believer's Portion - "Eternal Life."
(5) The Believer's Security - "Never Perish."

My sheep hear my voice . . . and they follow me: and I give unto them eternal life; and they shall never perish, neither shall any man pluck them out of my hand.

John 10:27, 28

NOAH'S CARPENTERS

Many hundred years ago
　　They ventured to remark
That Noah had some carpenters
　　To help him build the Ark.
But sad to say on that last day
　　When Noah entered in,
Those carpenters were left outside
　　And perished in their sin.

How sad to think they may have
　　Helped to build the Ark so great,
Yet still they heeded not God's Word
　　And awful was their fate.
Today the same sad fate exists
　　Among the sons of men, they
　　Help to build the so-called Church
　　Who are not born again.

They stay behind for sacrament,
　　They work, they sing, they pray;
Yet never have accepted Christ,
　　The Life, the Truth, the Way.
Another judgment day will come,
　　As sure as came the flood,
And only those will be secure
　　Who shelter 'neath Christ's Blood.

God's house is a hive for workers, not a nest for drones.	The less real religion a church has, the more bazaars and entertainment it takes to keep it going.
The church is not a refrigerator for perishable piety but a dynamo for charging men.	The key that unlocks heaven doesn't fit every church door.

Some people devote all their religion to going to church.	The church that is not a missionary church soon will be a missing church.
The best remedy for a sick church is to put it on a missionary diet.	You can't build a church with stumbling blocks.

VVVVVVVVVVVVVVVVVVVVVVVVVVVVVVVVVVVVVVVVVVVV

A CHURCH GARDEN

Three Rows of Squash
1. Squash indifference.
2. Squash criticism.
3. Squash gossip.

Four Rows of Turnips
1. Turn up for meetings.
2. Turn up with a smile.
3. Turn up with a visitor.
4. Turn up with a Bible.

Five Rows of Lettuce
1. Let us love one another.
2. Let us welcome strangers.
3. Let us be faithful to duty.
4. Let us truly worship God.
5. Let us give liberally.

AAAAAAAAAAAAAAAAAAAAAAAAAAAAAAAAAAAAAAAAAA

What the church needs is
less BLOCK
and
more TACKLE.

Ask yourself, "What kind of a church would ours be if everyone was like I am?"

Some churches seem to be sound in doctrine,
but they are sound asleep.

Some people have only three occasions for attending church: When they are hatched, matched, and dispatched.

Some people are like buzzards—they never go to church unless someone dies.

SOME DON'TS FOR CHURCH ATTENDERS

Don't visit; worship.

Don't hurry away; speak and be spoken to.

Don't dodge the preacher; show yourself friendly.

Don't dodge the collection plate; contribute what you are able.

Don't sit in the end of the pew; move over.

Don't stare blankly while others sing; join in.

Don't wait for an introduction; introduce yourself.

Don't criticize; remember your own frailties.

Don't monopolize your hymn book; be neighborly.

Don't stay away from church because you have company; bring them with you.

Don't stay away from church because the church is not perfect; how lonely you would feel in a perfect church.

THE EARLY CHURCH

A believing Church
An obedient Church
A steadfast Church
A praying Church
A worshiping Church
A joyful Church
A praising Church
An effective Church
A growing Church

The morning congregation is an indication of the popularity of the Church; the evening congregation is an indication of the popularity of the pastor; the prayer meeting attendance is an indication of the popularity of JESUS CHRIST!!

Enter expectantly,
Breathe prayerfully,
Worship reverently,
Relax restfully,
Greet others cordially
Leave thoughtfully,
Come again soon.

DICTIONARY OF CHURCH ATTENDERS

PILLARS — Worship regularly, giving time and money.

LEANERS — Use the church for funerals, baptisms, and marriages.

SPECIALS — Help and give occasionally for something that appeals to them.

ANNUALS — Dress up for Easter and come for Christmas programs.

SPONGES — Take all blessings and benefits, even the sacraments, but never give out anything themselves.

SCRAPPERS — Take offense and criticize.

COMFORT

I never knew a night so black,
Light failed to follow on its track;
I never knew a storm so gray,
It failed to have its clearing day.
I never knew such bleak despair,
That there was not a rift, somewhere;
I never knew an hour so drear,
Love could not fill it full of cheer.

J.K.B.

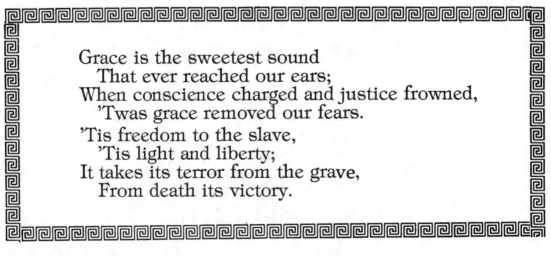

Grace is the sweetest sound
  That ever reached our ears;
When conscience charged and justice frowned,
  'Twas grace removed our fears.
'Tis freedom to the slave,
  'Tis light and liberty;
It takes its terror from the grave,
  From death its victory.

And Mary said, Behold the handmaid of the Lord; be it unto me according to Thy Word.   Luke 1:38

Anne Steele, whose hymns have helped so very many people, encountered much pain and sorrow as she journeyed through life. The evening before her wedding day, while waiting for the arrival of her betrothed, she received the message that he had been drowned. She retired to her room; and when the first violent shock has passed away and her soul had somewhat recovered strength, she wrote a hymn which has brought healing to many a wounded spirit:

Father, whate'er of earthly bliss Thy sovereign will denies;
Accepted at the throne of grace let this petition rise:
Give me a calm and thankful heart from every murmur free,
The blessing of Thy grace impart and let me live to Thee.

— Choice Gleanings

God does not COMFORT us
to make us COMFORTABLE,
but to make us COMFORTERS.

There is no sickness but there is a balm;
There is no storm but soon must come a calm;
No bitter wail but shall give way to a song;
No way so dark but light shall break e'er long.

COMMITMENT

OCCUPIED

Martha in the kitchen, serving with her hands;
Occupied for Jesus, with her pots and pans.
Loving Him, yet fevered, burdened to the brim,—
Careful, troubled Martha, occupied for Him.

Mary on the footstool, eyes upon her Lord;
Occupied with Jesus, drinking in His word.
This the one thing needful, all else strangely dim:
Loving, resting Mary, occupied with Him.

So may we, like Mary, choose the better part:
Resting in His presence—hands and feet and heart;
Drinking in His wisdom, strengthened with His grace;
Waiting for the summons, eyes upon His face.

When it comes, we're ready, spirit, will, and nerve;
Mary's heart to worship, Martha's hands to serve;
This the rightful order, as our lamps we trim,—
Occupied with Jesus, then occupied for Him!

—Lois Reynolds Carpenter

Rest in the Lord, my soul;
   Commit to Him thy way.
What to thy sight seems dark as night,
   To Him is bright as day.

Rest in the Lord, my soul;
   He planned for thee thy life,
Brings fruit from rain, brings good from pain,
   And peace and joy from strife.

Rest in the Lord, my soul;
   This fretting weakens thee.
Why not be still? Accept His will;
   Thou shalt His glory see.

God does not ask about our ability
or our inability,
but about our availability.

EVERYDAY MIRACLES
God, let me be content
  With simple things;
The twinkling of a star,
  A bird that sings,
The roaring of a wave,
  A sunset view,
A tiny blade of grass,
  A drop of dew,
Autumn's golden splendor,
  A flower fair,
The echo of a woods,
  A baby's stare,
The stillness of the night
  A sky of blue,
Memories to treasure,
  A friend that's true
A swallow's swift descent,
  A timid fawn,
A mother's loving care,
  The sun at dawn.
Simple things? Forgive my
  Human frailty!
Each one a miracle
  Revealing Thee!

—Francis H. O'Brien

This hope supports me in the storms,
    When flesh and spirit quail:
My Father holds me with His arm,
    His promise cannot fail.

The ocean of His grace transcends
    My small horizon's rim,
And where my feeble vision ends
    My heart can rest in Him.

In confidence I bide the tryst:
    His promise is for aye.
He guides me still, through cloud and mist,
    Unto the perfect day.

"It does not matter," said J. Hudson Taylor, "where He places me or how. That is rather for Him to consider than for me. For the easiest positions He must give grace; and in the most difficult His grace is sufficient. So, if God places me in great perplexity, must He not give me much guidance? in positions of great difficulty, much grace? in circumstances of great pressure and trial, much strength? As to work, mine was never so plentiful, so responsible, or so difficult; but the weight and strain are all gone. His resources are mine, for He is mine."

The fear of the Lord makes a hero; the fear of men makes a coward.

Resolved, to live with all my might while I do live. Resolved, never to lose one moment of time, to improve it in the most profitable way I can. Resolved, never to do anything which I should despise or think meanly in another. Resolved, never to do anything out of revenge. Resolved, never to do anything which I should be afraid to do if it were the last hour of my life.

Count your many obligations,
Name them one by one;
And it will surprise you
What the Lord wants done.

We leave it to Himself
To choose and to command;
With wonder filled, we soon shall see
How wise, how strong His hand.

THE LORD HAS NEED OF IT

Peter lent a boat,
To save Him from the press;
Martha lent her home,
With busy kindliness.

One man lent a colt,
Another lent a room;
Some threw down their garments,
And Joseph lent a tomb.

Simon lent his strength,
The cruel cross to bear;
Many brought their spices,
His body to prepare.

What have I to lend?
No boat, no house, no lands;
Dwell, Lord, within my heart.
I put it in Thy hands.

—Christ Life

"Birds of the air have made their nest,
And foxes in their holes find rest;
But I can offer you no bed;
No place have I to lay my head."

In shame I hung my head and cried,
How could I spurn the Crucified?
Could I forget the way He went,
The sleepless nights in prayer He spent?

For forty days without a bite,
Alone He fasted day and night.
Despised, rejected—on He went,
And did not stop till veil He rent.

A man of sorrows and of grief,
No earthly friend to bring relief—
"Smitten of God," the prophet said—
Mocked, and bruised, His blood ran red.

If He be God and died for me,
No sacrifice too great can be
For me, a mortal man, to make;
I'll do it all for Jesus sake.

Yes, I will tread the path He trod,
No other way will please my God;
So, henceforth, this my choice shall be
My choice for all eternity.

—Bill McChesney
Congo Martyr

MY CHOICE

I want my breakfast served at eight
With ham and eggs upon the plate.
A well-broiled steak I'll eat at "one"
And dine again when day is done.

I want an ultra modern home,
And in each room a telephone;
Soft carpets, too, upon the floors,
And pretty drapes to grace the doors.

A cozy place of lovely things,
Like easy chairs with innersprings.
And then, I'll get a small TV—
Of course, "I'm careful what I see."

I want my wardrobe, too, to be
Of neatest, finest quality.
With latest style in suit and vest.
Why shouldn't Christians have the best?

But then the Master I can hear,
In no uncertain voice, so clear,
"I bid you come and follow me,
The lowly Man of Galilee.

THE COST OF CONSECRATED LIVING

It cost ABRAHAM the yielding up of his son.
It cost DANIEL to be cast in the lions' den.
It cost STEPHEN death by stoning.
It cost PETER a martyr's death.
It cost PAUL to be beheaded.
It cost JESUS to die on the cross.
DOES IT COST YOU ANYTHING?

Tonight, my soul, be still and sleep;
The storms are raging on God's deep—
God's deep, not thine; be still and sleep;
Tonight, my soul, be still and sleep;
God's hand shall still the tempest's sweep—
God's hand, not thine; be still and sleep.

YESTERDAY is gone forever;
TOMORROW never comes;
God places the emphasis upon the NOW of TODAY.

George Muller's advice to those who desired to know the will of God:

1. Be slow to take new steps in the Lord's service, or in your business, or in your families. Weigh every thing well; weigh all in the light of the Holy Scriptures, and in the fear of God.

2. Seek to have no will of your own, in order to ascertain the mind of God regarding any steps you propose to take; so that you can honestly say you are willing to do the will of God, if He will only instruct you.

3. But when you have found out what the will of God is, seek for His help, and seek it earnestly, perseveringly, patiently, believingly, expectantly, and you will surely, in His own time and way obtain it.

T IS NOT EASY

To apologize,	To endure success,
To begin over,	To profit by mistakes,
To be unselfish,	To forgive and forget,
To take advice,	To think and then act,
To admit error,	To keep out of the rut,
To face a sneer,	To make the best of little,
To be charitable,	To subdue an unruly temper,
To keep on trying,	To maintain a high standard,
To be considerate,	To shoulder a deserved blame,
To avoid mistakes,	To recognize the silver lining—
	But it always pays.

—Ohio Educational Monthly

Some people are known by their deeds; Others by their mortgages.

When you THINK, when you SPEAK,
When you READ, when you WRITE,
When you SING, when you WALK,
When you seek for DELIGHT—
To be kept from all evil
At home and abroad, live always
As under the eye of the Lord.

When those I love from me depart to mansions in the skies,
And sorrow overwhelms the heart, and blinds my weeping eyes;
O Lord! let this my comfort be, that so it seemeth good to Thee.

COMPANIONSHIP

Thy speech bewrayeth thee.   Matt. 26:73

You tell on yourself by the friends you seek, by the very manner in which you speak; by the way you employ your leisure time, by the use you make of dollar and dime.

You tell what you are by the things you wear, by the spirit in which your burden you bear; by the manner in which you bear defeat, by so simple a thing as how you eat.

You tell what you are by the way you walk, by the things of which you delight to talk; by the book you choose from the well-filled shelf. In these ways and more you tell on yourself.

You and Christ together
Down the long, long trail,
Makes no difference whether
Road be hill or dale;
Fair or cloudy weather,
He will never fail;
You and Christ . . . TOGETHER
Down the long, long trail.

CONSISTENCY

Do what you can today,
you may not be here tomorrow.

The secret of success is consistency of purpose.

In essentials, UNITY;
In nonessentials, LIBERTY;
In all things, LOVE.

Live so your autograph will be wanted and not your fingerprints.

The diamond cannot be polished without friction, nor man perfected without trials.

Everywhere that Paul went,
he made some people GLAD,
some people SAD,
and some people MAD.

How seldom we weigh our neighbor in the same balance with ourselves.
—Thomas á Kempis

In the straight and narrow way the traffic is all one way.

Deal with the faults of others as gently as your own.

It is plainly in our living shown,
by slant and twist,
which way the wind has blown.

It is better to look ahead and prepare than to look back and regret.

Let another man praise thee, and not thine own mouth, a stranger and not thine own lips (Prov. 27:2).

So live that you wouldn't be ashamed to sell the family parrot to the town gossip.

Buy not silk
when you owe for milk.

Those who stand for nothing are apt to fall for anything.

Men are used as they use others.

A little more KINDNESS and a little less CREED;
A little more GIVING and a little less GREED;
A little more SMILE and a little less FROWN;
A little less KICKING a man when he's DOWN;
A little more "WE" and a little less "I";
A little more FLOWERS on the pathway of LIFE;
And FEWER on graves at the END OF THE STRIFE.

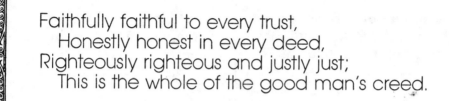

Faithfully faithful to every trust,
 Honestly honest in every deed,
Righteously righteous and justly just;
 This is the whole of the good man's creed.

It is not what we EAT
 but what we DIGEST
that makes us strong;
not what we GAIN
 but what we SAVE
that makes us rich;
not what we READ
 but what we REMEMBER
that makes us learned;
and not what we PROFESS
 but what we PRACTICE
that makes us Christians.

You will never have a friend if you seek one without faults.

The smallest good deed is better than the grandest intention.

If you growl all day, its natural to feel dog-tired at night.

Blessed is the man whose eyesight will stand as much reading in the Bible as in the Sunday paper.

Our words may hide our thoughts, but our actions will reveal them.

The secret of being a saint is being a saint in secret.

The reason a dog has so many friends is because he wags his tail instead of his tongue.

The best test of a man's doctrine is the application of it in his own life.

It is better to remain silent and appear dumb, than to speak and remove all doubt.

A coward can praise Christ, but it takes a man of courage to follow Him.

The voice of a holy life often speaks loudest when the tongue is silent.

There is no place to hide sin Without the conscience looking in!

Blessed is the man who is as much interested in the weekly prayer meeting as he is in social activities.

Blessed is the man who can adjust to a set of circumstances without surrendering his convictions.

**We have no right to sing:
"In the cross of Christ I glory"
unless we are willing to add,
"by whom the world is crucified
unto me and I unto the world."**

If the Lord intended for us to live in a permissive society, wouldn't the Ten Commandments have been the Ten Suggestions?

If you want the world to heed,
put your creed
in your deed.

Have the grace to say,
"I was WRONG
and you were RIGHT."

An easy conscience makes a soft pillow.

If you want to walk with God you must go God's way.

Tell me your company and I will tell you who you are.

The world doesn't need a definition of religion as badly as it needs a demonstration.

He who is born of God is certain to resemble his father.

Revenge is the sword that wounds the one who wields it.

A false balance is an abomination to the Lord;
but a just weight is his delight (Prov. 11:1).

And shall I use these ransomed powers of mine
For things that only minister to me?
Lord, take my tongue, my hands, my heart, my all,
And let me live and love and give for thee!

There are two parts to the Gospel:
believing it and behaving it.

The person who stays out of church because there are too many hypocrites in it, is doing the right thing; one more wouldn't improve the situation.

OUR WORDS
May hide our thoughts
BUT OUR ACTIONS
Will reveal them.

DON'T STAY AWAY FROM CHURCH BECAUSE—

YOU ARE POOR—there is no admission charge.

BECAUSE IT RAINS—you go to work in the rain.

BECAUSE IT IS HOT—it's hot at your house too.

BECAUSE IT IS COLD—it is always warm and friendly at church.

BECAUSE NO ONE INVITED YOU—people go to the movies without being begged.

BECAUSE WE HAVE AN EMOTIONAL RELIGION—how about the ball games?

BECAUSE YOU HAVE VERY SMALL CHILDREN—what if you didn't any longer have them?

YOU DON'T LIKE THE PREACHER—remember he's human like you.

YOUR JOB MAKES YOU SO TIRED—you could lose your job.

THERE ARE HYPOCRITES—you associate with them every day. You should be accustomed to them by now.

YOU HAVE COMPANY—they will admire your loyalty if you invite them along, or tell them to wait until you get back.

YOUR CLOTHES ARE NOT GOOD ENOUGH—we do not conduct a fashion show.

OUR CHURCH STANDARD IS TOO HIGH—just take a look at the Bible standard if you think ours is high.

YOU HAVE PLENTY OF TIME YET—ARE YOU SURE?

— Selected

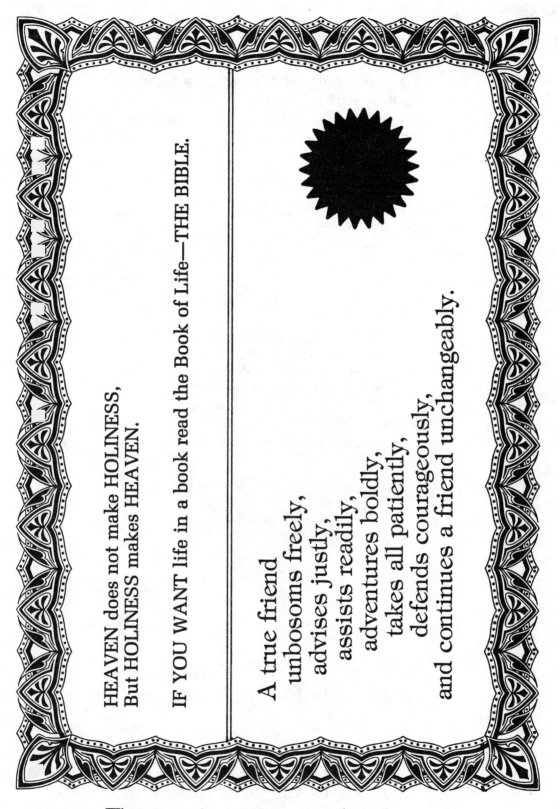

HEAVEN does not make HOLINESS,
But HOLINESS makes HEAVEN.

IF YOU WANT life in a book read the Book of Life—THE BIBLE.

A true friend
unbosoms freely,
advises justly,
assists readily,
adventures boldly,
takes all patiently,
defends courageously,
and continues a friend unchangeably.

**What we are is more important than what we say.
Our life is our best sermon.**

**To live above with saints we love,
O that will be glory!
To live below with saints we know,
That's a different story!**

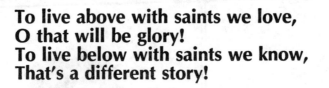

The question is not what a man can scorn,
Or disparage, or find fault with,
But what he can love, and value, and appreciate.
— John Ruskin

Remove far from me vanity and lies; give me neither poverty nor riches; feed me with food convenient for me; lest I be full, and deny thee, and say, who is the Lord? Or lest I be poor, and steal, and take the name of God in vain (Prov. 30:8-9)

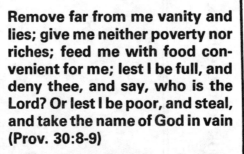

The man who walks with God always gets to his destination.

A QUITTER never wins,
and a WINNER never quits.

Thy soul must overflow
If thou another soul
would'st reach;
It needs the overflow of
heart
To give the lips full speech.

It is hard to pay for bread that has been eaten.

St. Francis of Assisi was hoeing his garden when someone asked what he would do if he were suddenly to learn that he would die before sunset. "I would finish hoeing my garden." he replied.

Wash your own windows
and see how clean
your neighbor's look.

If you don't live it, you don't believe it.

By the outward acts we can judge the inward thoughts.

An upright man
can never be
a downright failure.

You don't have to explain something you haven't said.

Before passing judgment on a sermon, be sure to try it out in practice.

A mountain has no need of words—
it says so much without them.
Thus should be our lives!

When men speak ill of you,
so live that no one will believe them.

A consistent Christian life is the best interpretation and proof of the Gospel.

Our walk must square with our talk.

Before you flare up at anyone's faults,
take time to count ten—
ten of your own.

A sound argument must have more than sound to it.

Fewer people would be in debt if they didn't spend what their friends think they make.

Blessed is the man who can sit as long on a hard pew in church as he can on a hard bleacher at a ball game.

MONEY WILL BUY

A bed but not sleep.
Books but not brains.
Food but not appetite.
Finery but not beauty.
A house but not a home.
Medicine but not health.
Luxuries but not culture.
Amusements but not happiness.
Religion but not salvation.

Be not angry that you cannot make others
as you wish them to be,
since you cannot make yourself
as you wish to be.

—Thomas á Kempis

Life is like a mirror—
if you frown at it,
it frowns back;
if you smile,
it returns the greeting.

If a man is too busy to worship
God twice on Sunday and once on
Wednesday night, he has more
business than God intended him
to have.

J. C. Penney

'Tis not enough to say, "I'm sorry and repent,"
And then go on from day to day just as I always went.
Repentance is to leave the sins we loved before,
And show that we in earnest grieve by doing them no more.

Be an "AMEN" Christian, but don't shout it
any louder than you live it.

He who fears God has nothing else to fear.

The person who is pulling on the oars
usually hasn't time to rock the boat.

**Where God's finger points,
God's hand will always make the way.**

People look at you six days in the week
to see what you mean on the seventh.

We can preach only the Christ that we live.

It is more important to watch how a man lives
than to listen to what he says.

**The best way to prove GODLINESS
is by GOD-LIKE-NESS.**

It isn't your position in life that counts—
it's your disposition.

If your spirit is grateful and humble,
then your tongue will not constantly grumble.

Blessed is the man whose eyesight will stand
as much reading in the Bible as in the
Sunday paper.

Be what your friends think you are;
avoid what your enemies say you are;
go right ahead and be happy.

CONTENTMENT

THE TWENTY-THIRD PSALM

The Lord is my Shepherd, I SHALL NOT WANT.

I shall not want REST. "He maketh me to lie down in green pastures."

I shall not want REFRESHMENT. "He leadeth me beside the still waters."

I shall not want FORGIVENESS. "He restoreth my soul."

I shall not want GUIDANCE. "He leadeth me in the paths of righteousness, for His name's sake."

I shall not want COMPANIONSHIP. "Yea, though I walk through the valley of the shadow of death, I will fear no evil, for Thou art with me."

I shall not want COMFORT. "Thy rod and thy staff they comfort me."

I shall not want FOOD. "Thou preparest a table before me in the presence of my enemies."

I shall not want JOY. "Thou anointest my head with oil."

I shall not want ANYTHING. "My cup runneth over."

I shall not want ANYTHING IN THIS LIFE. "Surely goodness and mercy shall follow me all the days of my life."

I shall not want ANYTHING IN ETERNITY. "And I will dwell in the house of the Lord forever."

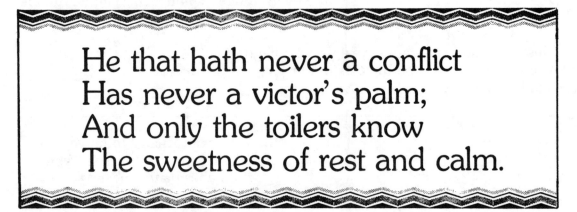

He that hath never a conflict
Has never a victor's palm;
And only the toilers know
The sweetness of rest and calm.

Contentment consists not
in great wealth,
but in few wants.

Contentment is finding as many
benefits for not getting what we
want as we do for getting what
we want.

He that's content hath enough.
He that complains has too much.

He shall cover thee with his feathers, and under his wings shalt thou trust: his truth shall be thy shield and buckler (Ps. 91:4).

What a great trial! "The terror by night"; "the pestilence that walketh in darkness"; "the destruction that wasteth at noonday." The whole day and night! (Ps. 91:5, 6).

What a great trust! Under His wings. The mother bird covers the young birds with her feathers and thus they find warmth and shelter. Under these wings the young find safety. Our Lord would have gathered unbelieving Jerusalem under His wings as the mother bird does but they would not. I would — ye would not. (Matt. 23:37). How sad!

Under His wings I am safely abiding
Though the night deepens and tempests are wild,
Still I can trust Him, I know He will keep me,
He has redeemed me, and I am His child.

—Choice Gleanings

Sometimes the Lord calms the storm;
sometimes He lets the storm rage and
calms His child.

Those hands are still outstretched to bless,
His people's wayward feet to guide,
Till dawn shall break and shadows flee,
When He will come to claim His bride.
Then in those saint-thronged courts above,
From every clime and every land,
With wondering joy we'll look on Him
Who bore the nailprints in His hand.

— Choice Gleanings

It is right to be content with what you have,
but not with what you are.

You don't have to go places
if you are happy where you are.

A contented mind is a continual feast.

Fortify yourself with contentment,
for this is an impregnable fortress.
—Epicetus

Every person lives in one of two tents:
conTENT or disconTENT.
In which do you live?

Discontent makes rich men poor, while
contentment makes poor men rich.

REST

It is such rest to know
The while my bark is tossed on billow's foam—
Now high, now low—
That raging seas can never overwhelm,
Because my Father's hand is on the helm
To pilot me safely HOME.

HIS SECURITY

Jesus Christ is no security against storms,
But He is a perfect security in storms.
He has never promised an easy passage,
Only a safe landing.

All His saints are in thy hand.   Deut. 33:3

We're in His hand, that mighty hand, that flung a universe in space . . . That guides the sun and moon and stars, and holds the planets in their place . . . We're in His hand, that skillful hand, that made the blinded eyes to see . . . That touched the leper, cleansed and healed, and set the palsied sufferer free . . . We're in that hand, that loving hand that lifted children to His breast . . . That fed the hungry multitudes and beckoned weary hearts to rest . . . We're in His hands, those pierced hands, once nailed to Calvary's cruel tree . . . When there in agony and blood He paid the price to set us free.

FOR A CONTENTED LIFE

Health enough to make work a pleasure.

Wealth enough to support our needs.

Strength to battle with difficulties and overcome them.

Grace enough to confess our sins and forsake them.

Patience enough to toil until some good is accomplished.

Charity enough to see some good in your neighbor.

Love enough to move you to be useful and helpful to others.

Faith enough to make real the things of God.

Hope enough to remove all anxious fears concerning the future.

CONVERSATION

That which lies in the well of your thought will come up in the bucket of your speech.

It is the shallow brook
   that babbles.

Some people ought to be sent to solitary confinement.

Great minds discuss ideas
Average minds discuss events
Small minds discuss people.

CONVICTION

THE PUSSYFOOTER

A preacher, anxious to be strong in his preaching without offending anyone said something like this:

"If you do not repent, as it were; and be converted, in a measure; you will go to hell, to a certain extent."

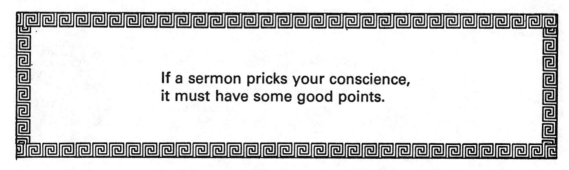

If a sermon pricks your conscience,
it must have some good points.

COOPERATION

We can see that life is a cycling phenomenon
which occurs in many forms within a single system.
Nothing stands alone—no individual, species,
or community; no rain drop, snow crystal, cloud,
or stream; no mountain and no sea—for in a cycle
each thing in one way or another
is connected with everything else.

COURAGE

Courage isn't a brilliant dash,
A daring deed in a moment's flash;
It isn't an instantaneous thing
Born of despair with a sudden spring.
But it's something deep in the soul of man
That is working always to serve some plan.
— Edgar A. Guest

Keep your fears for yourself,
but share your courage with others.
— Robert Louis Stevenson

COURTESY

BEATITUDES FOR FRIENDS OF THE AGED

Blessed are they that understand
My faltering step and palsied hand.
Blessed are they that know my ears today
Must strain to catch the things they say.
Blessed are they who seem to know
That my eyes are dim and my wits are slow.
Blessed are they that look away
When the coffee spilled at the table today.
Blessed are they with a cheery smile
Who stop to chat for a little while.
Blessed are they who never say,
"You've told that story twice today."
Blessed are they who find the way
To bring back memories of Yesterday.
Blessed are they who make it known
That I'm loved and not alone.
Blessed are they who ease the days
On my journey Home in loving ways.
—Esther Mary Walker

A little oil of courtesy will save a lot of friction.	Never speak loudly to one another unless the house is on fire.
The greater the man, the greater the courtesy.	Nothing costs so little and goes so far as Christian courtesy.
Courtesy is a duty the servants of Christ owe to the humblest person on earth.	The measure of a truly great man is the courtesy with which he treats small men.

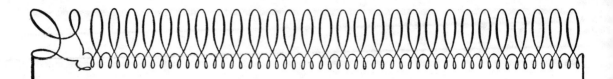

Everybody knows how to express a COMPLAINT but few can utter a graceful COMPLIMENT.

A GRACIOUS WORD is an EASY OBLIGATION.

Study the language of gentleness; Refuse words that bite, and tunes that crash.

How sweet and gracious even in common speech is that sense which men call courtesy.

Life is not so short but that there is always time for courtesy.

Courtesy is a science of the highest importance which ought to be on the curriculum of every Christian.

If we must DISAGREE, let us not be DISAGREEABLE.

CRITICISM

When looking for faults, use a MIRROR not a TELESCOPE

Nothing is easier than fault-finding:
it takes no talent,
no self-respect,
no brains,
no character,
to set up the grumbling business.

Nobody raises his own reputation by lowering others.

It is easy to acquire the fault-finding habit but it is hard to be liberated from it.

Criticism can be avoided by
saying nothing,
doing nothing,
and being nothing.

How seldom we weigh our neighbor in the same balance with ourselves.
—Thomas á Kempis

God has given us two ears, two eyes, and one tongue, to the end that we should hear and see more than we speak.

Worse than the sin you criticize is the sin of criticism.

The man who is always finding fault seldom finds anything else.

A KNOCKER never wins; A WINNER never knocks

It is much easier to be critical than to be correct.

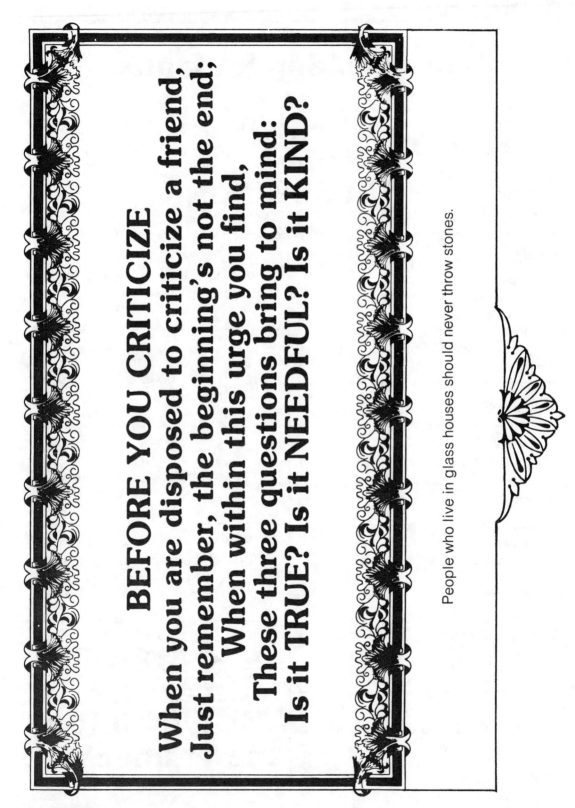

BEFORE YOU CRITICIZE

When you are disposed to criticize a friend,
Just remember, the beginning's not the end;
When within this urge you find,
These three questions bring to mind:
Is it TRUE? Is it NEEDFUL? Is it KIND?

People who live in glass houses should never throw stones.

DON'T CRITICIZE
your wife's judgment—
See whom she married!

GREAT SPIRIT,
teach me never to judge another
until I've walked
at least two weeks in his moccasins.
—An Indian Prayer

A mule makes no headway when he is kicking;

neither does a man.

All loud speakers are not necessarily hooked up.

If you are criticized,
you have either done something worthwhile,
or refrained from doing something foolish.
So, CONGRATULATIONS!

CRITICISM
comes easier than
CRAFTSMANSHIP

DETERMINATION

CONSIDER THE HAMMER—
It keeps its head.
It doesn't fly off the handle.
It keeps pounding away.
It finds the point and then drives it home.
It looks at the other side, too,
and thus often clinches the matter.
It makes mistakes, but when it does,
it starts all over.
It is the only knocker in the world
that does any good.

Some people grin and bear it.
Others smile and change it . . .

Even the woodpecker owes his success to the fact that he uses his head and keeps pecking away until he finishes the job he starts.	How shall we conquer if we do not fight? —Wesley
Some people never change their opinion because it has been in the family for generations.	Once to every man and nation comes a moment to decide in the strife of truth and falsehood, for the good or evil side.
A dead fish can float down stream, but it takes a live fish to swim upstream.	Lincoln was great, not because he lived in a log cabin, but because he was able to get out of it.

WHAT IS A SQUARE?

Everybody knows a few squares. I know one. He's that strong, polite, God-fearing young fellow who freely admits that he prays, weeps for joy, plays with little kids, kisses his mother, goes to his dad for advice, and thinks old folks are great. He wears clothes that fit him, puts savings in the bank, has his hair neatly groomed, likes school, can't imitate all the television comics, avoids dirty discussions about sex — he even blushes. He goes to church, drinks milk, drives within the speed limit, is in bed by 12, doesn't smoke, and expects purity in girls.

As a result of his unusual behavior, he suffers the loss of gang companionship; but he gains the gratitude and admiration of his parents, family, and teachers, has an unjaded imagination, and enjoys spiritual perception. To some he may seem a strange fellow, but I like him!

—Anon.

It isn't the
SIZE OF THE DOG IN THE FIGHT
but the
SIZE OF THE FIGHT IN THE DOG
that determines which wins.

LINCOLN'S ROAD TO THE WHITE HOUSE
Failed in business in 1831
Defeated for legislature in 1832
Second failure in business in 1833
Suffered a nervous breakdown in 1836
Defeated for Speaker in 1838
Defeated for Elector in 1840
Defeated for Congress in 1843
Defeated for Congress in 1848
Defeated for Senate in 1855
Defeated for Vice President in 1856
Defeated for Senate in 1858
Elected President in 1860

*Nothing is impossible
to a willing soul.*

No greater champion
than the man
who conquers a
bad habit.

*Do what you may,
DOGS will bark
and ASSES bray.*

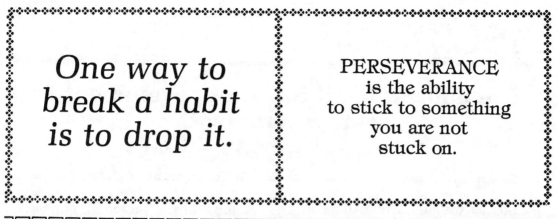

One way to break a habit is to drop it.

PERSEVERANCE is the ability to stick to something you are not stuck on.

MY CREED

To live as gently as I can;
To be, no matter where, a man;
To take what comes of good or ill
And cling to faith and honor still;
To do my best, and let that stand
The record of my brain and hand;
And then, should failure come to me,
Still work and hope for victory.

To have no secret place wherein
I stoop unseen to shame or sin;
To be the same when I'm alone
And when my every deed is known;
To live undaunted and unafraid
Of any step that I have made;
To be without pretense or sham
Exactly what men think I am.

To leave some simple mark behind
To keep my having lived in mind;
If enmity to aught I show,
To be an honest, generous foe,
To play my little part, nor whine
That greater honors are not mine.
This, I believe, is all I need
For my philosophy and creed.

— Edgar Guest

DISCIPLINE

The noblest of all forms of government is self-government, but it is the most difficult.

Chasten thy son while there is hope, and let not thy soul spare for his crying (Prov. 19:18).	A good father, finding his son on the wrong track, will provide switching facilities.
The rod and reproof give wisdom: but a child left to himself bringeth his mother to shame (Prov. 29:15).	It is less painful to DISCIPLINE a child than to WEEP OVER a spoiled youth.
On Sunday morning it is often a debate between ought and auto.	
Withhold not correction from the child: for if thou beatest him with the rod, he shall not die (Prov. 23:13).	

Everything nowadays is controlled by switches —except children.

He who reigns within himself,
and rules passions, desires, and fears,
is more than a king.

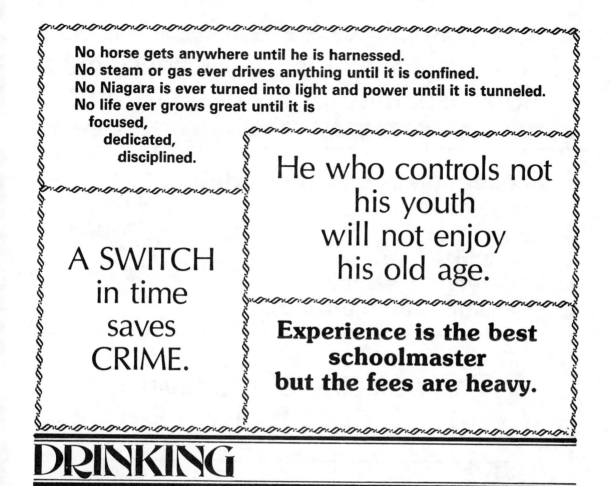

No horse gets anywhere until he is harnessed.
No steam or gas ever drives anything until it is confined.
No Niagara is ever turned into light and power until it is tunneled.
No life ever grows great until it is
focused,
dedicated,
disciplined.

A SWITCH
in time
saves
CRIME.

He who controls not
his youth
will not enjoy
his old age.

**Experience is the best
schoolmaster
but the fees are heavy.**

DRINKING

The hand that lifts "the cup that cheers"
should not be used to shift the gears.

The driver is safer when the roads are dry.
The roads are safer when the driver is dry.

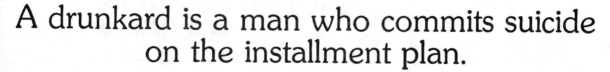

A drunkard is a man who commits suicide
on the installment plan.

The booze-dealer is the business man who is ashamed of his best customer.

Alcohol makes a man colorful:
  it gives him;
  a red nose,
    a white liver,
      a yellow streak
        and a blue outlook.

The best side of the tavern is the outside.

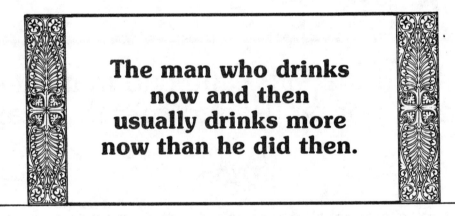

The man who drinks now and then usually drinks more now than he did then.

The gunman wants "your money or your life,"
but the tavern keeper takes both.

Wine is a mocker, strong drink is raging, and whosoever is deceived thereby is not wise (Prov. 20:1).

A DRUNK is the past tense of a DRINK

It takes about 1500 nuts
to hold an auto together,
but it takes only one nut
to scatter it over the road.

The man who enters the bar
very optimistically
often comes out very
mistoptically.

A swerving car—a driver drunk
A heavy crash—a pile of junk!
A wrecking car—a doctor by
A frightened child—a wife's sad cry!
An orphan child—a widow lone;
A new-made grave where pine trees moan!
A tragic thing—may we repeat
A tragic thing—a drunk's moment!

EGOTISM

"All the world,"
said the Quaker to his wife,
"is queer,
except me and thee,
and even thee is a
little queer."

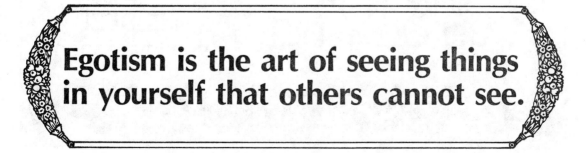

Egotism is the art of seeing things in yourself that others cannot see.

One who boasts of his ancestry
is like the potato:
the best part of him
is under the ground.

A CONCEITED PERSON has one good point. He doesn't talk about OTHER PEOPLE.

He who parades
his virtues
seldom leads
the parade.

Some people are like a
toy balloon:
a pin prick and
there is nothing left of them.

Some people grow under responsibilities;
others merely swell.

Some self-made men show poor architectural skill.

An EGOTIST
is a person
who is always
ME-DEEP
in conversation.

Conceit may puff a man up, but it will never prop him up.

Every way of a man is right in his own eyes; but the Lord pondereth the hearts (Prov. 21:2).

Seest thou a man in his own conceit? There is more hope of a fool than of him (Prov. 26:16).

When it comes to self, we look more for men's approval than for needed correction and help.

How to stay ignorant:
Be SATISFIED
with your own opinions,
and CONTENT
with your own knowledge.

If you think you have no fault, that is possibly the worse one.

Some folks would rather blow their own horn than to listen to Sousa's band.

You're always in the wrong key when you start singing your own praises.

If some men would lose their self-conceit, there wouldn't be much left of them.

One of the hardest secrets for a man to keep is his opinion of himself.

I had a little tea party
  This afternoon at three
'Twas very small—
  Three guests in all—
Just I, myself, and me.
  Myself ate all the sandwiches,
While I drank up the tea.
  'Twas also I who ate the pie
And passed the cake to me.

An EGOTIST
is an
"I" SPECIALIST

Pride is like a man's shirt,
it is the first thing on,
and the last thing off.

Don't permit your feelings to be hurt;
that is only a form of egotism.

Show me a thoroughly satisfied man,
and I will show you a failure.
—Thomas A. Edison

How much we admire the wisdom
of those who come to us for advice.

Some people boast of being self-made men.
That relieves God of a great responsibility.

Few love to hear
of the sins
they love to act.

To entertain some people
all you have to do
is listen.

ETERNITY

ONE SHORT LIFE for watching with the Master,
   ETERNAL YEARS to walk with Him in white,
ONE SHORT LIFE to bravely meet disaster,
   ETERNAL YEARS to reign with Him in light,
ONE BRIEF LIFE for weary toils and trials,
   ETERNAL YEARS for calm and peaceful rest,
ONE BRIEF LIFE for patient self-denials,
   ETERNAL YEARS for life, where life is best.

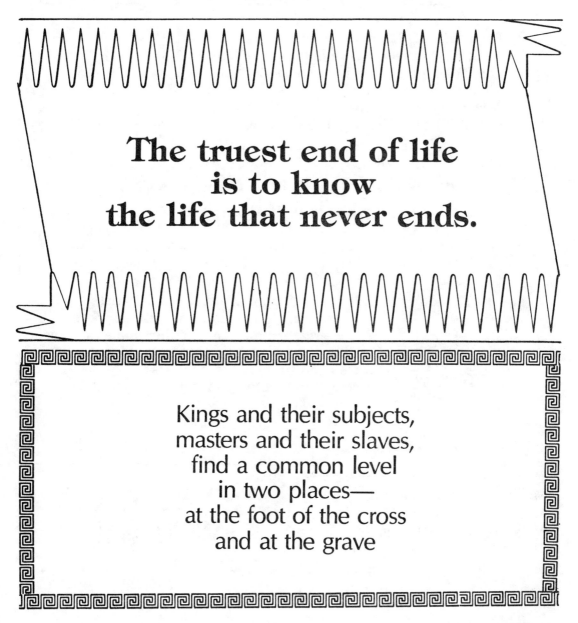

The truest end of life is to know the life that never ends.

Kings and their subjects,
masters and their slaves,
find a common level
in two places—
at the foot of the cross
and at the grave

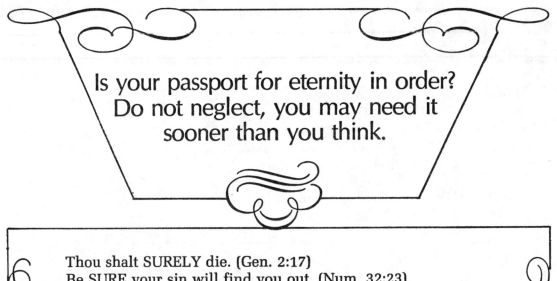

Is your passport for eternity in order?
Do not neglect, you may need it
sooner than you think.

Thou shalt SURELY die. (Gen. 2:17)
Be SURE your sin will find you out. (Num. 32:23)
The foundation of the Lord standeth SURE. (II Tim. 2:19)
We have also a more SURE word of prophecy. (II Peter 1:19)
A hope both SURE and stedfast. (Heb. 6:19)
SURELY I come quickly. (Rev. 22:20)

Life with Christ is an endless hope;
without Him it is a hopeless end.

WORK FOR ETERNITY

If we work upon marble, it will perish;
If we work upon brass, time will efface it;
If we rear temples, they will crumble into dust;
But—if we work upon immortal souls
we engrave upon these tablets
something that will brighten all eternity.

As a tree falls so must it lie,
As a man lives so must he die,
As a man dies so must he be
All through the days of eternity.

ETERNITY!
WHERE?

EVANGELISM

It is finished!
NOTHING, either great or small—
NOTHING, sinner, no NOTHING;
Jesus did it, DID IT ALL,
Long, long ago!

LORD, lay some soul upon my heart,
and love that soul through me,
and may I nobly do my part
to win that soul for Thee.

A RECIPE FOR A REVIVAL

If all the SLEEPING folks would WAKE UP
And all the LUKEWARM would FIRE UP
And all the DISGRUNTLED would SWEETEN UP
And all the DISCOURAGED would CHEER UP
And all the DEPRESSED would LOOK UP
And all the ESTRANGED would MAKE UP
and all the GOSSIPERS would SHUT UP
Then there might come a revival.

— Selected

The difference between catching men and catching fish: you catch fish that are alive and they die, but you catch men that are dead and they are brought to life.

EXAMPLE

25 THINGS WE CAN'T DO

1. Sow bad habits and reap a good character.
2. Sow jealousy and hatred and reap love and friendship.
3. Sow wicked thoughts and reap a clean life.
4. Sow wrong deeds and live righteously.
5. Sow crime and get away with it.
6. Sow dissipation and reap a healthy body.
7. Sow crooked dealings and succeed indefinitely.
8. Sow self-indulgence and not show it in your face.
9. Sow disloyalty and reap loyalty from others.
10. Sow dishonesty and reap integrity.
11. Sow profane words and reap clean speech.
12. Sow disrespect and reap respect.
13. Sow deception and reap confidence.
14. Sow untidiness and reap neatness.
15. Sow intemperance and reap sobriety and temperance.
16. Sow indifference and reap nature's rewards.
17. Sow mental or physical laziness and reap a responsible position in society.
18. Sow cruelty and reap kindness.
19. Sow wastefulness and reap thriftiness.
20. Sow cowardice and reap courage.
21. Sow destruction of other people's property and reap protection for our own.
22. Sow greed and envy and reap generosity.
23. Sow neglect of the Lord's house and reap strength in temptation.
24. Sow neglect of the Bible and reap a well-guided life.
25. Sow human thistles and reap human roses.

—James Nankivell

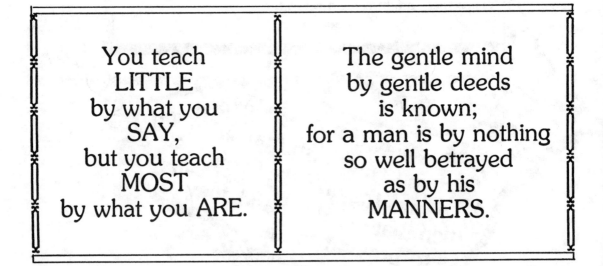

You teach
LITTLE
by what you
SAY,
but you teach
MOST
by what you ARE.

The gentle mind
by gentle deeds
is known;
for a man is by nothing
so well betrayed
as by his
MANNERS.

A prince who was traveling in the care of his tutor, asked how he ought to act under such and such circumstances. "Always remember that thou art a king's son," said the tutor.

GOD'S MINORITIES

During the time NOAH was building the ark, he was very much in the minority — but he won!

When JOSEPH was sold into Egypt by his brothers, he was a decided minority — but he won!

When GIDEON and his three hundred followers, with their broken pitchers and lamps, put the Midianites to flight they were in an insignificant minority — but they won!

When ELIJAH prayed down fire from heaven and put the prophets of Baal to shame, he was in a notable minority — but he won!

When DAVID, ridiculed by his brothers, went out to meet Goliath, in size he was in a decided minority — but he won!

When MARTIN LUTHER nailed his theses on the door of the cathedral he was a lonesome minority — but he won!

When JESUS CHRIST was crucified by the Roman soldiers, he was a conspicuous minority — but he won!

Others will follow your footsteps more easily than they will follow your advice.

Ye are manifestly declared to be the epistle of Christ ministered by us, written not with ink, but with the Spirit of the living God; not in tables of stone, but in fleshy tables of the heart.

II Cor. 3:3

What does the unsaved world learn when it reads us? Is the letter clear and distinct, or blotted and blurred? Do the unsaved have a clearer vision of Christ, or is their opinion of Him lessened by what little of Him they see written in our lives and attitudes?

—G. M. Landis

A careful man I ought to be,
A little fellow follows me.
I do not dare to go astray,
For fear he'll go the selfsame way.
Not once can I escape his eyes;
Whate'er he sees me do he tries.
Like me he says he's going to be,
That little chap who follows me.
I must remember as I go
Through summer sun and winter snow,
I'm molding for the years to be—
That little chap who follows me.

The light that shines farthest
shines brightest at home.

The author is known by his writings,
a fool by his words,
and all men by their companions.

You can preach a better sermon
with your life
than with your lips.
—Goldsmith

"Beloved, now are we the sons
of God, and it doth not yet appear what we shall be."
— I John 4:17

FAITH

No man has ever tested the resources of God until he tries the human impossible.	The devil hasn't armies enough to capture one saint of God who dares to trust Him.
Faith in God makes the uplook good, the outlook bright, and the future glorious.	Faith in God is a perfect antidote for the fear of men and the creed of circumstances.
If fear knocks at the door, let faith go to open it, and no one will be there.	*A traveler crossed a frozen stream* *In trembling fear one day;* *Later a teamster drove across,* *And whistled all the way.*
Let us have the faith that right makes might, and in that faith let us dare to do our duty.	*Great faith and little faith alike* *Were granted safe convoy;* *One had the pangs of needless fear,* *The other all the joy.*

FAITH IS
a higher faculty than reason

Faith makes all things possible and love makes them easy.
Faith either removes mountains or tunnels through.
The greatness of our fear shows us the littleness of our faith.
It is impossible for faith to overdraw its account in God's bank.
Faith believes the Word of God for what it cannot see, and is rewarded by seeing what it believes.

FAITH IS
believing what God says simply because it is God who says it.

None live so pleasantly as those who live by faith.

God gives a promise that we may take by faith.

Men lightly drop a faith they feebly hold.

Living without trust is like driving in a fog.

DOUBT sees the obstacles;
　FAITH sees the way.
DOUBT sees the darkest night;
　FAITH sees the day.
DOUBT dreads to take a step;
　FAITH soars on high.
DOUBT questions, "Who believes?"
　FAITH answers, "I".

*Every place that the sole of your foot shall tread upon, that have
I given unto you.　　　Josh. 1:3*

*This is possession by appropriation; by faith and fighting. This
was possessing their possessions. The promise of God to Abraham had given the inheritance to all his seed. The land was all
theirs. But they did not actually possess it till they set their foot
upon it. Many of our blessings are ours practically in the same
way. They are given to us in Christ but until faith sets its foot
upon them in appropriation they are not truly ours.　　　—L.S.*

Choice Gleanings

Tomorrow's plans I do not know,
　I only know this minute;
But He will say, "This is the way,
　By faith walk ye in it."

*At the close of his will Patrick Henry stated: There is one thing
more that I would like to leave to my family—Christian faith.
With that they would be rich did I not leave them one shilling.
Without that they would be poor had I given them the whole
world.*

Faith is a grasping of almighty power;
The hand of man laid hold on the arm of God;
The grand and blessed hour
In which the things impossible to me
Become the possible, O Lord, through Thee.

Faith is the assurance that the
thing God has said in His Word
is true.
and that God will act according
to what He has said in His Word.

FAITH IS
the tendril
by which the soul
clings to GOD.

The beginning of anxiety
is the end of faith,
and the beginning of true faith
is the end of anxiety.

— George Mueller

FAITH IS
a laboratory course—
not a lecture course.

Having got all wrinkled up with care and worry,
it's a good time to get your faith lifted.

FAITH IS
a principle by which to live,
and not a problem to be solved.

Faith
  sees the invisible,
    believes the incredible,
      and receives the impossible.

Ask yourself,
Does my faith remove mountains
or do mountains move my faith?

Act faith,
and it will bring results.

Faith alone saves,
but the faith that saves
  is not alone.

FAITH IS
far more a way of walking
than it is of talking

FAITH IS
saying Amen to God.

Trust God without terms.

FAITH IS
the gateway of communion with God.
LOVE IS
the gateway of ministry to men.

Fear not tomorrow, God is already there.

A firm faith in the promises of God is the best theology.

FAITH IS the soul's intake.
LOVE IS the soul's outlet.

FAITH

It cost ABRAHAM the yielding up of his son.
It cost DANIEL to be cast in the lion's den.
It cost STEPHEN death by stoning.
It cost PETER a martyr's death.
It cost JESUS His life.
DOES IT COST YOU ANYTHING?

Faith expects from God what is beyond all expectation.

**If we desire an increase of faith,
we must consent to its testings.**

Faith and fear can never exist together.

**Little faith will bring your soul to heaven,
but great faith will bring heaven to your soul.**

FAITHFULNESS

The Fate of the Apostles. . .

St. Matthew suffered martyrdom by being slain with a sword at a distant city of Ethiopia.

St. Mark expired at Alexandria, after having been cruelly dragged through the streets of that city.

St. Luke was hanged upon an olive tree in the classic land of Greece.

St. John was put into a caldron of boiling oil, but escaped death in a miraculous manner, and was afterwards banished to Patmos.

St. Peter was crucified at Rome with his head downward.

St. James the Greater was beheaded at Jerusalem.

St. James the Less was thrown from a lofty pinnacle of the temple, and then beaten to death with a fuller's club.

St. Philip was hanged up against a pillar at Heiropolis in Phrygia.

St. Bartholomew was flayed alive.

St. Andrew was bound to a cross, where he preached to his persecutors until he died.

St. Thomas was run through the body with a lance at Coromandel in the East Indies.

St. Jude was shot to death with arrows.

St. Matthias was first stoned, and then beheaded.

St. Barnabas of the Gentiles was stoned to death by the Jews at Salonica.

St. Paul after various tortures and persecutions, was at length beheaded at Rome by the Emperor Nero.

—Schumacher.

There has never been a statue erected to the memory of someone who left well enough alone.

You can do anything you want to, if you want to do what you ought to do.

My Lord knows the way through the wilderness. All I have to do is follow.

Behavior is the mirror in which everyone shows his image.

It is not success that God rewards but always the faithfulness of doing His will.

The greater danger for most of us is not that our aim is too high and we miss it, but that it is too low and we reach it.

Consider the postage stamp. Its usefulness lies in the ability to stick to one thing until completed.

God measures our gifts not by the greatness of them, but by the self-denial they express in giving them.

To get the true measure of a man's capacity, note how much more he does than is required of him.

Count that day lost whose low descending sun views from thy hand no worthy action done.

If we are faithful, God will look after our success.

God's part we cannot do; our part He will not do.

Be a stand-by for your church and not merely a by-stander.

No matter how stony the path, some forge ahead; no matter how easy the going, some lag behind.

The man who is worse than a quitter is the man who is afraid to begin.

It is human to stand with the crowd. It is divine to stand alone.

Blessed is the man who is too busy to worry in the day and too tired to lie awake at night.

Occasionally someone will say, "Our pastor never stops to visit in our home." If the pastor never stops at your home, you probably should thank God. It means death has not struck, that no serious illness has laid you low, or that the surgeon's knife had not been necessary, or that you have had no serious family problem or that you are not a spiritually delinquent member. As a rule, your pastor does not have time for "social calls." It is not that he would not enjoy doing so, it is simply a matter of priorities . . . putting first things first. Your pastor does not have time to do everything he would like to do. However, you may be sure of this: your pastor is willing to come to the hospital or your home, the jail, the street corner, or anywhere at any hour of the day, or night when he is needed. Call him if you need him. Otherwise he will not know of your need until it is too late. For the moment, thank God you have not needed him. One day you will need him and he will be there when you call. Now he is visiting someone else who does need him.

**True courage is like a kite:
a contrary wind raises it higher.**

I have only just a minute,
Just sixty seconds in it;
Forced upon me—can't refuse it,
Didn't seek it, didn't choose it;
I must suffer if I lose it,
Give account if I abuse it,
Just a tiny little minute,
But eternity is in it.

Every day that dawns brings something to do that can never be done well again.

When faithfulness is most difficult, it is most rewarding.

The world crowns success, but God crowns faithfulness.

Busy persons are not busybodies.

A politician thinks of his next election— a statesman thinks of his next generation.

You may depend on the Lord, May He depend on you?

Some pay their bills when due,
Some never do.
And how do you do?

A tree does not fall at the first stroke.

Even the smallest undertaking is worth the pains of good workmanship.

Faithfulness in little things is a great thing.

Anyone can CARRY HIS BURDEN,
however hard, until nightfall.
Anyone can DO HIS WORK,
however hard, one day.
Anyone can live SWEETLY, PATIENTLY, LOVINGLY,
until the sun goes down.
And this is all that life really is.

Robert Louis Stevenson

> God has His best things for the few
> Who dare to stand the test,
> He has His second choice for those
> Who will not have His best.

FAITHFULNESS

When Stanley went out in 1871 and found Livingstone, he spent some months in his company, but Livingstone never spoke to Stanley about spiritual things. Throughout those months Stanley watched the old man. Livingstone's habits were beyond his comprehension, and so was his patience. He could not understand Livingstone's sympathy for the Africans. For the sake of Christ and His Gospel, the missionary doctor was patient, untiring, eager, spending himself and being spent for his Master. Stanley wrote, "When I saw that unwearied patience, that unflagging zeal, those enlightened sons of Africa, I became a Christian at his side, though he never spoke to me about it.

A. Naismith

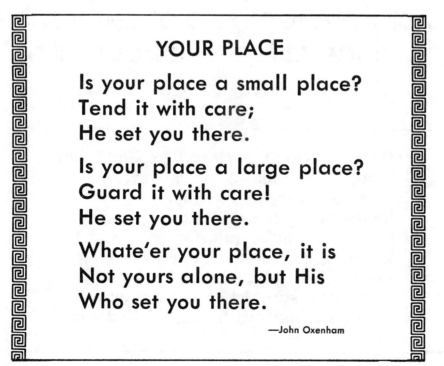

YOUR PLACE

Is your place a small place?
Tend it with care;
He set you there.

Is your place a large place?
Guard it with care!
He set you there.

Whate'er your place, it is
Not yours alone, but His
Who set you there.

—John Oxenham

What is that in thine hand?   Exod. 4:2

"What is that in thy hand, Abel?" "Nothing but a wee lamb, O God, I purpose offering it to Thee, a willing sacrifice." And so he did, and the sweet smell of that burning has been filling the air ever since. "What is that in thy hand, Moses?" "Nothing but a staff, O God, with which I tend my flocks." "Take it and use it for Me." And so he did, and it wrought more wondrous things than Egypt had ever seen before. "Mary, what is that in thy hand?" "Nothing but a pot of precious ointment, O God, wherewith I would anoint Thy Holy Son." And so she did, and the perfume filled the house, and has ever since been a memory of her. "Poor woman, what is that thou hast in thy hand?" "Only two mites, Lord, and I would give it to Thee." And she has ever since inspired others to give to the Lord.

E. Barker

Shamgar had an ox-goad, David had a sling,
Dorcas had a needle, Rahab had some string,
Samson had jawbone, Moses had a rod,
Mary had some ointment but they all were
   used of God.

—Choice Gleanings

It's not the greatness of our troubles, but the littleness of our faith that makes us complain.

Who does God's work will get God's pay,
However long may seem the day,
However weary be the way.
He does not pay as others pay,
In gold or land or raiment gay,
In goods that perish and decay.
But God's highest wisdom knows the way:
And that is sure, let come what may,
Who does God's work will get God's pay.

When He enquires, "Where wroughtest thou?
Account to Me, My servant, now."
Shall I be able then to say that I have wrought in
any way?
That I have sacrificed my ease to let my answer
be like these:

> "I, Lord? Beneath the tropic sun I won lost
> souls for Thee."
> "I? In the Sunday school I sought Thy servant,
> Lord, to be."
> "I? In the home; Thou didst Thyself appoint
> that place for me."
> "I? For Thy saints like Epaphras, I toiled on
> bended knee."

Spin carefully,
Spin prayerfully,
But leave the threads
with God.

I am only one,
but I am one.
I cannot do everything,
   but I can do something.
And what I can do
   I ought to do
and by the grace of God
   I WILL DO IT.

Each one of us has got a niche;
Lord, help me to discover which,
That when Thou comest and dost ask:
"Child, where didst thou perform thy task?"
My answer may be:
"By Thy grace I filled my God-appointed place."

What you
CAN DO
you
OUGHT TO DO,
and what you
OUGHT TO DO,
by the help of God
DO!

Keep waiting
ON HIM
keep working
WITH HIM
keep watching
FOR HIM.

Each morning sees some task begun,
Each evening sees its close;
Something attempted, something done
Has earned a night's repose.

—Longfellow

Have a purpose in life,
and having it,
throw into your work
such strength
of mind and muscle
as God has given you.

Depend on it—
God's work
done in
God's way,
will never lack
God's supplies.

Be like the watch:
have an open face,
busy hands,
full of good works,
pure gold, and
well regulated.

The gold that came from Thee, Lord,
To Thee belongeth still;
Oh, may I always faithfully
My stewardship fulfil.

The branch that bears the most fruit hangs the lowest.

Believe there is nothing too small to do well.

I have no YESTERDAYS,
Time took them away;
TOMORROW may not be—
But I have TODAY.

A talebearer revealeth secrets; but he that is of a faithful spirit concealeth the matter. Where no counsel is, the people perish: but in the multitude of counselors there is safety (Prov. 11:13, 14).

It is better to wear out than to rust out.

Man's idea of eternity may be known by the use he makes of time.

To know God's will is life's greatest treasure.
To do God's will is life's greatest pleasure.

Do you know that the church is a workshop and not a dormitory?

ENERGY and PERSISTENCE conquer all things

God has no larger field for the man who is not faithfully doing his work where he is.

Someone once asked Francis of Assisi how he was able to accomplish so much. He replied, "This may be why: The Lord looked down from Heaven and said, 'Where can I find the weakest, littlest man on earth?' Then He saw me and said, 'I've found him. I will work through him, and he won't be proud of it. He'll see that I am only using him because of his insignificance.' "

— From Our Daily Bread

FOOLS

Who learns and learns,
and acts not on what he learns,
is like the one
who plows and plows,
but never sows.

Only a FOOL
FOOLS with sin.

Wise men talk because they have something to say;
Fools talk because they just have to say something.

Many a man counted a fool by financiers has laid up in heaven fortunes they covet.

Seest thou a man who is hasty in his words? There is more hope of a fool than of him (Prov. 12:23).

A fool may have a knowing look, but it's all off when he opens his mouth.

Arguing with a fool shows there are two.

He is no fool who gives what he cannot keep to gain what he cannot lose.
— *Jim Elliot*

He who will not learn except of himself has a fool for a teacher.

FORGIVENESS

LET US TAKE TIME

To give God worship, service, and communion.
To live with our friends while we have them.
A coffin is a poor place for the warm handclasp and the cheery greeting.
To forgive our enemies. Jesus found time to do it between the blows of the hammer.
To go slower up hill when we are young, and down hill when we are old.

FRIENDLINESS

Being friends
   is a warm and glowing touch.
It's words
   of kindness that mean so much.
Through days
   and years that bond has grown.
A blessing
   only friends have known.
Being friends
   holds a meaning true,
It's past
   and present and yet it's new.
It's time
   wrapped up in things we do . . .
I'm glad
   God made a friend like you!

Emily Bertha Green

Friends, like all good things in this life, can be had by any one who wants them. There is only one simple rule to follow; it is this: to have a friend, be one yourself.

Few men have the natural strength to honor a friend's success without envy.

It is possible to disagree and still be agreeable.

Have no friends you dare not bring home.

Of all things you wear your expression is the most important.

The reason a dog has so many friends is because he wags his tail instead of his tongue.

All people smile in the same language.

A true friend is one who knows all about you and loves you just the same.

A friend is a present you give yourself.
— Robert Louis Stevenson

It's nice to be important, but more important to be nice.

A hedge between keeps friendships GREEN.

Friendships cemented together with sin don't hold.

The only way to have a friend is to be one.

Prosperity begets friends, Adversity proves them.

Promises may get friends, but it is performances that keep them.

A man that has friends must show himself friendly: but there is a friend that sticketh closer than a brother.
—Prov. 18:24

Choose your friends for what they are, and not by what they have.

A sign on a neighbor's front door: ENTER without knocking LEAVE the same way.

He who ceases to be your friend never was a good one.

Prosperity begets friends, Adversity proves them.

Your needy friend may some day be a friend in need.

True friends are like DIAMONDS, precious but rare.
False friends are like AUTUMN LEAVES, found everywhere.

GIVING

Man does not
OWN
his wealth;
he OWES it.

GIVING
is the
thermometer
of our love.

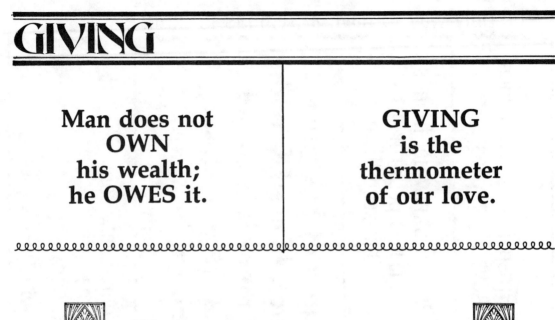

There is more power
in the
OPEN HAND
than in the
CLENCHED FIST.

You can give without loving,
but you can't love without giving.

Charity gives itself rich;
covetousness hordes itself poor.

The Lord loveth a cheerful giver—
until he brags about it.

Honour the Lord with thy substance, and with the first-fruits of all thy increase: so shall thy barns be filled with plenty, and thy presses shall burst out with new wine. (Prov. 3:9, 10).

Giving should be based on principle, regulated by system, beautified by self-sacrifice.

Not what we get, but what we give, measures the worth of the life we live.

Happy is the man who has learned to hold the things of this world with a loose hand.

It may be more blessed to give than to receive, but the average man is always willing to let the other fellow have the blessing.

First give yourself to God, then giving your possessions will be easy and joyful.

Someone said, "If you don't give according to your means, God will see that your means are according to your giving."

Give, though your gift be small, still be a giver;
Out of the little fount proceeds the river;
Out of the river's gifts gulfs soon will be
Pouring their waters out, making a sea.
Out of the sea again Heaven draws its showers,
And to the fount imparts all its new powers.
Thus in the circle born, gifts roll around,
And in the blessings given, blessing is found.

It is a common saying that a hog is good for nothing while he is alive. He cannot be ridden like the horse; he cannot be used to draw like the ox; he does not provide clothing like the sheep, nor milk like the cow; he will not guard the house like the dog. He is good only for the slaughter. So a covetous rich man, just like a hog, doth no good with his riches whilst he liveth; but when he is dead, his riches come to be disposed of.

There are three kinds of givers — the flint, the sponge and the honeycomb. To get anything out of the FLINT you must hammer it. And then you get only chips and sparks.
To get water out of a SPONGE you must squeeze it, and the more pressure you use, the more you will get.
But the HONEYCOMB just overflows with its own sweetness.

A lot of money is tainted—
'taint yours,
'taint mine,
but 'tis God's.

Giving advice to the poor is about as near charity as some people get.

Many people give the tenth—
the tenth of what they ought to give.

Jacob had no church to support, and the Jews no world to evangelize, and they gave the tithe.

He that hath pity upon the poor lendeth unto the Lord; and that which he hath given will He pay again.

There is that scattereth, and yet increaseth; and there is that withholdeth more than is meet, but it tendeth to poverty. The liberal soul shall be made fat; and he that watereth shall be watered also himself (Prov. 11:24, 25).

Give as you would to the Master
If you met His searching look;
Give as you would of your substance
If His hand the offering took.

The person who lives close to God
will not be close with God.

You can't take your money to heaven
but you can send it on ahead.

Selfishness with much can do little,
but love with little can do more.

When the heart is converted,
the purse will be inverted.

Of great riches there is no use,
except in distribution.

If you want to be rich—
GIVE!
If you want to be poor—
GRASP!
If you want abundance—
SCATTER!
If you want to be needy—
HOARD!

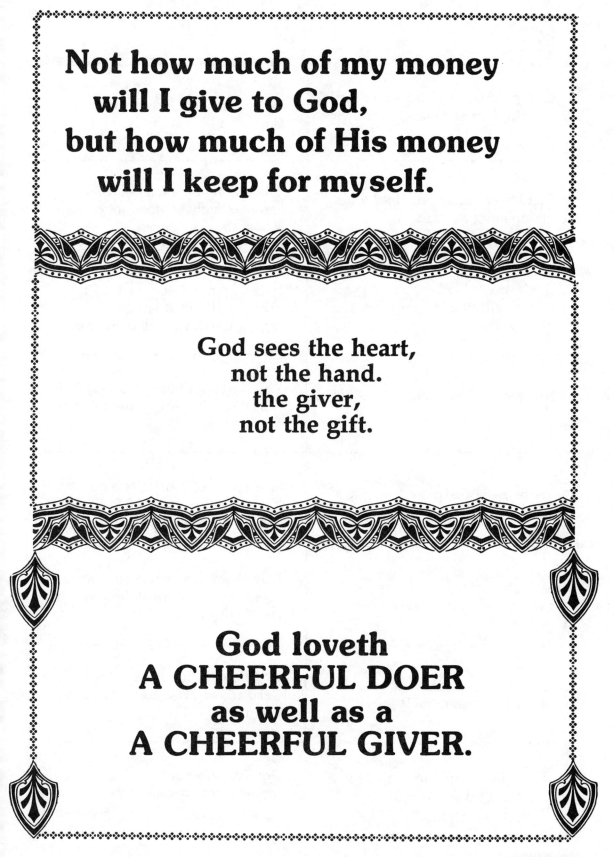

Not how much of my money
will I give to God,
but how much of His money
will I keep for myself.

God sees the heart,
not the hand.
the giver,
not the gift.

God loveth
A CHEERFUL DOER
as well as a
A CHEERFUL GIVER.

GOD

God provides food for every bird but He does not place it in their nest.	He who makes God first will find God with him at the last.
God never closes one door without opening another.	**There is nothing God will not do through one who does not care to whom the credit goes.**
Don't treat God as a lawyer, never calling Him until you are in trouble.	It is important to speak to men about God, but it is more important to speak to God about men.
No enemy can come so near that God is not nearer.	**The lot is cast into the lap; but the whole disposing thereof is of the Lord (Prov. 16:33).**
The peace of God passeth all understanding and misunderstanding.	The cross of Christ reveals the love of God at its best and the sin of men at its worst.
Only he who sees the invisible can do the impossible.	**God chastens us with many instruments, but they are all held in His ever-loving hand.**
In order to mould His people, God often has to melt them.	If God could speak through Balaam's ass, He surely can speak through you.
If you have God's promise for a thing, isn't that enough?	**God loves each one of us, as if there was only one of us.** —Augustine

HIS MERCIES ARE GREAT.   II Sam. 24:14

How great is His mercy! There is nothing little about God. He forgives great sins to great sinners after great lengths of time; gives great favors and great privileges and raises us up to great enjoyments in the great Heaven of the Great God.

— C. H. Spurgeon

Canst thou take the barren soil
And with all thy pains and toil
Make lilies grow?
Thou canst not; O helpless man,
HAVE FAITH IN GOD, HE CAN!
Canst thou paint the clouds at eve,
And all the sunset colors weave
Into the sky?
Thou canst not; O powerless man,
HAVE FAITH IN GOD, HE CAN!
Canst thou still thy troubled heart,
And make all cares and doubts depart
From out thy soul?
Thou canst not; O faithless man,
HAVE FAITH IN GOD, HE CAN!

Though doubt and dismay should enfold you,
And hope and relief become dim,
Remember that someone has told you
To "CAST ALL YOUR CARE UPON HIM."
If sorrow or trouble o'er take you,
And grief fills your cup to the brim,
There is one who will never leave you,
Then "CAST ALL YOUR CARE UPON HIM."

ALL THINGS are of God in their FOREORDINATION.
ALL THINGS are of God in their ORIGINATION.
ALL THINGS are of God in their PERPETUATION.
ALL THINGS are of God in their CONSUMMATION.

God wants men,
    but He does not need them;
Men need God,
    but they do not want Him.

While our heavenly Father does not promise a comfortable journey, He does guarantee a safe landing.

If you will be all God wants you to be, then you can do all God wants you to do.

He who abandons himself to God will never be abandoned by God.

Many people believe in God, but not many believe God.

One of the greatest evidences of God's love to those who love Him is to send afflictions with grace to bear them.

God never commands and commissions without providing grace to obey.

It is equally easy for God to supply our greatest as well as our smallest wants, to carry our heaviest as well as our lightest burden — just as the ocean bears the battleship as easily as it does the fisherman's vessel.

GOD'S WORK
must be done in
GOD'S WAY.

"God meant it unto good"
No second cause I see,
For 'tis my God appoints each day,
And plans my life for me.

He knows the burden of each heart,
He sees each falling tear;
He can the truest peace impart
In place of doubt and fear.
He watches o'er me constantly,
He knows my feeble frame;
His keeping power, His faithful love
Are evermore the same.

Got any rivers you think are uncrossable?
Got any mountains you can't tunnel through?
God specializes in things thought impossible.
And He can do what no other can do.

If God is on our side, what matters who is against us?	A quiet time with God is worth a life-time with men.
# Little is much if God is in it.	Whenever a man is ready to uncover his sins, God is always ready to cover them.
I do not know what is in the future, but I do know who is in the future.	Never despair: man's extremity is God's opportunity.
God is as great in minuteness as He is in magnitude.	A dewdrop does the will of God as much as the thunder storm.

God be in my HEAD,
And in my UNDERSTANDING;
God be in my EYES,
And in my LOOKING;
God be in my MOUTH,
And in my SPEAKING;
God be in my HEART,
And in my THINKING;
God be at my END,
And at my DEPARTING.

God looks down from His majestic throne on you. Amid the infinite variety of His works you are not overlooked. Amid the nobler services of ten thousand times ten thousand saints and angels, not one of your fervent prayers or groans escapes His ear. What a God! What a Savior! What a Lover!

Nothing with God is accidental.

Our great matters
are little to God's power.

God is BEFORE me, He will be my guide;
God is BEHIND me, no ill can betide;
God is BESIDE me, to comfort and cheer;
God is AROUND me, so why should I fear?

There is an arm that never tires
When human strength gives way;
There is a love that never fails
When earthly loves decay:
That arm upholds the worlds on high;
That love is throned beyond the sky.

We cannot always see the way
Where Thou, our gracious Lord, dost move;
But we can always surely say,
    That God is love.
When clouds hang o'er our darkened path,
We'll check our dread, each doubt reprove;
For here each saint sweet comfort hath,
    That God is love.

I love to think that God appoints
My portion day by day;
Events of life are in His hand,
And I would only say,
"Appoint them in Thine own good time
And in Thine own good way."

He knows, He loves, and cares—
Nothing this truth can dim—
And does the very best for those
Who leave the choice with Him.

God formed us,
sin deformed us,
but God alone
can transform us.

Do God's will at any cost.

When you have nothing left but God,
then for the first time you become aware that God is enough.

GOD gives His very best to those who leave the choice with Him.

With God one is never lost in the crowd.

God guides our STOPS as well as our STEPS.

God writes with a pen that NEVER BLOTS:
He speaks with a tongue that NEVER SLIPS;
He acts with a hand that NEVER FAILS.

As sure as God puts His children into the furnace of affliction, He will be with them there.

In spite of what God knows about us, and that is more than we know about ourselves, He loves us.

Where God guides,
He provides.

Let nothing disturb thee,
Nothing affright thee;
All things are passing;
God never changeth;
Patient endurance
Attaineth to all things;
Who God possesseth
In nothing is wanting;
Alone God sufficeth.

Longfellow

He cannot have taught us to trust in His name, and brought us thus far to put us to shame.

— J. Hudson Taylor

THAT UNSEEN EYE
There is an eye that never sleeps
Beneath the wings of night;
Soul, guard thy ways and words today
For thou art in His sight!

DEPEND UPON IT —
God's work,
done in God's way,
will never lack God's supplies.

J. Hudson Taylor

THREE GATES

If you are tempted to reveal
A tale to you someone has told
About another, make it pass,
Before you speak, three gates of gold.
These narrow gates: First, "Is it true?"
Then, "Is it needful?" In your mind
Give truthful answer. And the next
Is last and narrowest, "Is it kind?"
And if to teach your lips at last
It passes through these gateways three,
Then you may tell the tale, nor fear
What the result of speech may be.

— from The Arabian

Scandal is like an egg, when hatched it has wings.

A tongue
three inches long
can ruin a man
six feet tall.

"They say" is a tough old liar.

A gossip
is a person
with a strong sense
of rumor.

Plant a little gossip and you will reap a harvest of regret.

A loose tongue may get a person into a tight place.

Gossip always seems to travel fastest over grapevines that are slightly sour.

A groundless rumor often covers a lot of ground.

Silence is an excellent remedy against slander.

A dog is loved by old and young, he wags his tail and not his tongue.

Nothing pays smaller dividends in spiritual results than making a specialty of talking of the shortcomings of others.

Gossip is anything that goes in one ear and over the back fence.

Where no wood is, there the fire goeth out, so where there is no talebearer, the strife ceaseth (Prov. 26:20).

Gossip is sharing private information with those who are not part of the problem or part of the solution.

To speak ill of others is only a round about way of bragging about yourself.

Remember, running people down is bad business, whether you are a motorist or a gossip.

The gossip's stock is largely hearsay—and what they don't hear, they say anyway.

Men, like fish, would be safer if they kept their mouth shut.

The only person who makes a success in running people down is the elevator boy.

GREATNESS

If you want to get UP, step DOWN.
If you want to be SEEN, get out of SIGHT.
If you want to be GREAT, forget YOURSELF.

To belittle is to be little,
to be grateful is to be great.

The beginning of greatness is to be little,
the increase of greatness is to be less,
and the perfection of greatness is to be nothing.

The heights by great men reached and kept
Were not attained by sudden flight,
But they, when their companions slept,
Were toiling upward in the night.

—Longfellow

The greatest truths
are the simplest;
so are men
and women.

A GRATEFUL mind
is a GREAT mind.

We can see that life is a cycling phenomenon
which occurs in many forms within a single system.
Nothing stands alone—no individual, species,
or community; no raindrop, snow crystal, cloud,
or stream; no mountain and no sea—for in a cycle
each thing in one way or another
is connected with everything else.

HABITS

Don't get in the habit of telling people where to get off unless you are a bus driver.

The chains of habit are too small to be felt until they are too strong to be broken.

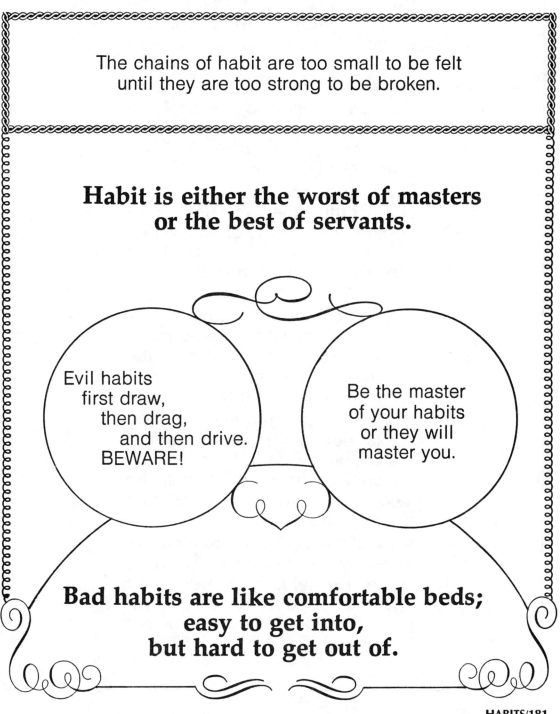

Habit is either the worst of masters or the best of servants.

Evil habits
first draw,
then drag,
and then drive.
BEWARE!

Be the master
of your habits
or they will
master you.

Bad habits are like comfortable beds; easy to get into, but hard to get out of.

HAPPINESS

WHERE IS HAPPINESS?

Not in unbelief—
Voltaire was an infidel of the most pronounced type. He wrote: "I wish I had never been born."

Not in pleasure—
Lord Byron lived a life of pleasure, if anyone did. He wrote: "The worm, the canker, and the grief are mine alone."

Not in money—
Jay Gould, the American millionaire, had plenty of that. When dying he said: "I suppose I am the most miserable man on earth."

Not in position and fame—
Lord Beaconsfield enjoyed more than his share of both. He wrote: "Youth is a mistake; manhood, a struggle; old age, a regret."

Not in military glory—
Alexander the Great conquered the known world in his day. Having done so, he wept, because, he said, "There are no more worlds to conquer."

Where, then, is happiness found? The answer is simple: In Christ alone. He said, "I will see you again, and your heart shall rejoice, and your joy no man taketh from you."

Cheerfulness oils the machinery of life.

Happiness is not perfected until it is shared.

Happiness is a perfume you cannot pour on others without getting a few drops on yourself.

Cheerfulness greases the axles of the world.

Happiness increases the more you spread it around.

True happiness consists in making others happy.

Blind But Happy

O what a happy soul am I!
    Although I cannot see,
I am resolved that in this world
    Contented I will be;
How many blessings I enjoy
    That other people don't!
To weep and sigh because I'm blind
    I cannot, and I won't.

—Fanny Crosby (8 years old)

There are two essentials to happiness: something to do, and someone to love.

It is not how much we have but how much we enjoy what we have that makes happiness.

While seeking happiness for others we consistently find it for self.

All the handmade keys in the world cannot unlock true happiness.

The secret of contentment is knowing how to enjoy what you have.

The year's at the spring
The day's at the morn;
Morning's at seven:
The hillside's dew-pearled;
The lark's on the wing;
The snail's on the thorn;
God is in His heaven—
All's right with the world.

—Robert Browning

It is easier to smile than to frown. It takes 64 muscles of the face to frown, only 13 to smile.	A merry heart maketh a cheerful countenance; but by sorrow of heart the spirit is broken (Prov. 15:13).
A smile is mightier than a grin.	Money is a universal provider for most everything but happiness, and a universal passport to most any place but heaven.

He is the happiest, be he king or peasant, who finds peace in his home.

If place I choose or place I shun,
My soul is satisfied with none;
But when Thy will directs my way,
'Tis equal joy to go or stay.

HEAVEN

A man may go to heaven without health, without wealth, without fame, without a great name, without learning, without culture, without friends, without ten thousand other things. But he can never go to heaven without Christ!

The countless multitude on high,
That tune their songs to Jesus' Name,
All merit of their own deny,
And Jesus' worth alone proclaim.
Firm on the ground of sovereign grace,
They stand before Jehovah's throne;
The only song in that blest place
Is, "Thou art worthy! Thou alone!"
— Choice Gleanings

The love of heaven makes one heavenly.

HOME, the pilgrim's toil is o'er; how sweet the rest . . . A voice from heaven declares that such are blessed . . . HOME, amid radiant hosts of saints in light . . . HOME, with the SAVIOR, faith now lost in sight . . . HOME, in the Father's house of joy untold . . . HOME, where His glories to our eyes unfold . . . HOME, blessed Home to praise Him evermore . . . HOME, yes at home, forever to adore . . . HOME, where His love would have us near His side . . . HOME, with HIMSELF forever to abide.

BUILDING OUR OWN MANSION

There is a legend of a wealthy woman who, when she reached heaven, was shown a very plain mansion. She objected. "Well," she was told, "that is the house prepared for you." "Whose is that fine mansion across the way?" she asked. "It belongs to your gardener." "How is it that he has one so much better than mine?" "The houses here are prepared from the materials that are sent up. We do not choose them, you do that by your earthly faithfulness."
(This may be a legend, but it bears a profound truth.)

In heaven above, Marys and Marthas will weep no more because a brother dies. There will be no Rachels weeping for their children because they are not. Broken ties will be reknit; lost links will be found again; all hearts will be bound together and no heart will break, for we shall be where there is fullness of joy and pleasures for evermore.

H. K. Downie

Soon where earthly beauty blinds not, no excess of brilliance palls,
Salem, city of the holy, we shall be within thy walls!
There, beside yon crystal river, there, beneath life's wondrous tree,
There, with naught to cloud or sever—ever with the Lamb to be.

— H. Bonar

God has two thrones: one in highest heaven and the other in the lowest heart.

What we weave in this world we shall wear in heaven.

In this dark world of sin and pain
We only meet to part again;
But when we reach the heavenly shore,
We there shall meet to part no more;
The joy that we shall see that day
Shall chase our present griefs away.

Nature is like an outstretched finger pointing up toward heaven.

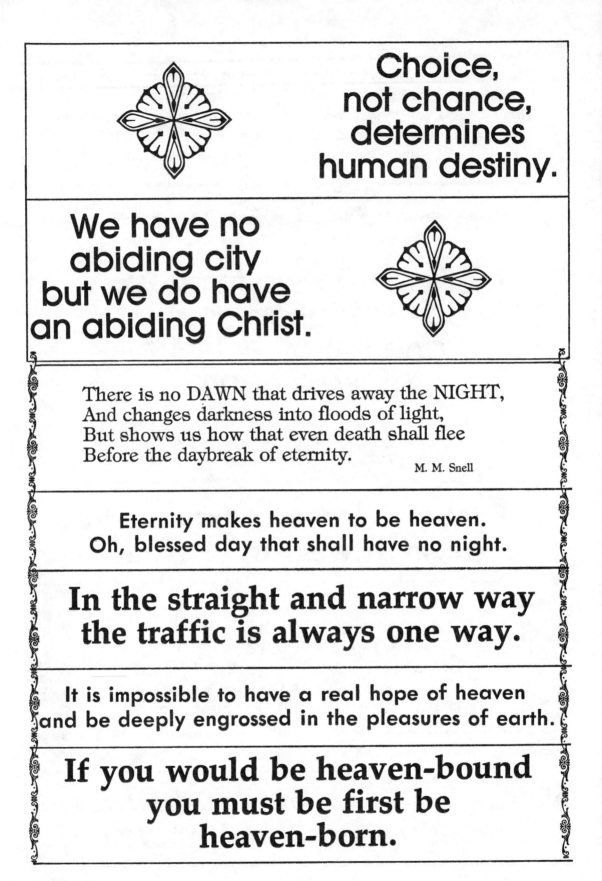

Choice,
not chance,
determines
human destiny.

We have no
abiding city
but we do have
an abiding Christ.

There is no DAWN that drives away the NIGHT,
And changes darkness into floods of light,
But shows us how that even death shall flee
Before the daybreak of eternity.

M. M. Snell

Eternity makes heaven to be heaven.
Oh, blessed day that shall have no night.

In the straight and narrow way
the traffic is always one way.

It is impossible to have a real hope of heaven
and be deeply engrossed in the pleasures of earth.

If you would be heaven-bound
you must be first be
heaven-born.

All the darkness will be past when I get home,
And the crown of life at last, when I get home.
I shall stand before Him;
Gladly I'll adore Him;
Ever to be with Him when I get home.

It is only a little while, Christian,
  Till all labors and trials shall cease;
And, instead of heartaches and sorrows
  There shall be a wonderful peace.
The Savior is coming to claim thee,
  He is now preparing your home;
When trials beset thee, oh, whisper,
  'Twill only be thus till He come.

He who is on the road to heaven will not be content to go there alone.

He who seldom thinks of heaven
is not likely to be
on his way to heaven.

When the shore is won at last, who will count the billows past?

A COUNTRY CALLED HEAVEN

I want to tell you of a strange and wonderful country, a country where there are no tears or heartaches, a country in which there is no sickness, pain or death. The people who live in this country never get tired. They carry no burdens and they never grow old. No one ever says good-bye, for separations are unknown, and there are no disappointments.

In the country of which I am speaking, there is no sin, for no one ever does wrong. There are no accidents of any kind. You will travel for thousands of miles and never see a cemetery or meet a funeral procession. There are no undertakers and no morgues. You will never see crepe on the doors, for no one ever dies. There they need no gravediggers and coffins are unknown. The clothes that are worn are bright and glistening and no one dresses in mourning.

It is a country where nothing ever spoils. The flowers never lose their fragrance and the leaves are always green. There are no thunderstorms, no erupting volcanoes, and no earthquakes. Upon those fair shores hurricanes and tidal waves never beat. There are no germs or fevers, no pestilence of any kind. The sun never shines and yet it is always light for there is no night there. It is never too hot and never too cold. The temperature is exactly right. No clouds ever darken the sky and harsh winds never blow.

There are no drunkards in this country for no one ever drinks. None are immoral; men as well as women are pure. There are no illegitimate babies. Prisons, jails and reformatories never darken the landscape. Doors have no locks and windows no bars, for thieves and robbers never enter there. No

lustful books are read, and as for unclean pictures, they are never seen. No taxes are paid and rents are unknown. It is a country free from war and bloodshed.

Yes, and let me tell you something else. There are no cripples to be seen anywhere; none are deformed or lame. Nor is anyone blind, deaf or dumb; hence, homes for incurables have never been built for all are healthy, all are well and strong. No beggars are seen on the streets for none are destitute and all have enough. Leprosy and cancer, palsy and tuberculosis are words that this country has never heard. No asylums are there, for none are feeble minded. Doctors are never needed and hospitals are unknown.

You ask me how I know all this? Have I been there? No, I have not yet had the privilege of visiting this wonderful country, but others have. And One, at least, who has lived there for a long, long time, has come, and told me a great deal about it. He says it is called heaven, and this is His description of it: "Behold, the tabernacle of God is with men, and he will dwell with them, and they shall be his people, and God himself shall be with them and be their God. And God shall wipe away all tears from their eyes, and there shall be no more death, neither sorrow, nor crying, neither shall there be any more pain." (Rev. 21:3-4).

Do you want to go there? Then get ready now. It isn't difficult. All you have to do is to open your heart to Jesus Christ, the Lord of the country, and ask Him to come in. Then, when the journey of life is ended, you too will go to this wonderful country and dwell there for ever more. Will you do it? Do it — NOW?

—Oswald J. Smith

HELL

Grant that hell fire is but a symbol of the punishment which awaits the unbelieving: in what respects have they who have persuaded themselves of this improved their prospects?

The man who tries to prove there is no hell, generally has a personal reason for doing so.

You tell me you don't believe in hell; let me tell you that five minutes after you've been there, you will.

There is an exit sign in public buildings almost everywhere—but there are no EXIT signs in hell.

HONOR LOST — much lost;
LIFE LOST — more lost;
SOUL LOST — all lost.

As sure as night follows day
and winter follows summer,
so shall wrath follow sin.

There is a way to stay out of hell.
but no way to get out.

Hell is paved with good intentions.

HEREAFTER

MY PRAYER FOR YOU

The Lord preserve thy GOING OUT,
The Lord preserve thy COMING IN;
God send His angels round about
To keep thy soul from every sin,
And when thy GOING OUT is done,
And when thy COMING IN is o'er,
When in death's darkness all alone,
Thy feet can COME and GO no more,
The Lord preserve thy GOING OUT
From this dark world of sin and grief,
While angels standing round about
Sing, "God preserve thy COMING IN."

Rest in the Lord, and wait patiently for him.   Ps. 37:7
Be silent to God, and let Him mold thee. (Luther's literal translation).

From vintages of sorrow are deepest joys distilled,
And the cup outstretched for healing is oft at Marah filled;
God leads to joy through weeping, and to quietness through strife;
Through yielding unto conquest, through death to endless life.
Be still! He hath enrolled thee for the kingdom and the crown.
Be silent! Let Him mold thee, who calleth thee His own.

Be still, my soul, the hour is hastening on
    When we shall be forever with the Lord;
When disappointment, grief, and fear are gone,
    Sorrow forgot, love's purest joys restored.
Be still, my soul! When change and tears are past,
All safe and blessed we shall meet at last.

—Choice Gleanings

SINCE YESTERDAY

Along the golden streets
A stranger walks tonight
With wonder in his heart—
Faith blossomed into sight.

He walks and stops and stares,
And walks and stares again.
Vistas of loveliness
Beyond the dreams of men.

He who once was weak,
And often shackled to a bed,
Now climbs eternal hills
With light and easy tread.

He has escaped at last
The cruel clutch of pain;
His lips shall never taste
Her bitter cup again.

O never call him dead,
This buoyant one and free,
Whose daily portion is
Delight and ecstacy!

He bows in speechless joy
Before the feet of Him
Whom, seeing not, he loved
While yet his sight was dim.

Along the golden streets
No stranger walks today,
But one who, long homesick,
Is home at last, to stay!

—Martha Snell Nicholson

The lights are all out
  In the mansion of clay;
The curtains are drawn,
  For the dweller's away;
She silently slipped
  O'er the threshold by night,
To make her abode
  In the City of Light.

Psalm 23:4 is often misquoted by mentioning "a dark valley." But the word "dark" is not there. It says, "the valley of the SHADOW of death." There can be no shadow in a dark place. The fact that there is shadow shows that there is a light in the valley. All death can do is to throw a shadow over the place. Shadows never hurt anyone. We have nothing to fear.

Light after darkness, gain after loss;
Strength after weakness, crown after cross;
Sweet after bitter, hope after fears;
Home after wandering, praise after tears;
Sheaves after sowing, sun after rain;
Sight after mystery, peace after pain;
Joy after sorrow, calm after blast;
Rest after weariness, sweet rest at last;
Near after distant, gleam after gloom;
Love after loneliness, life after tomb;
After long agony, rapture of bliss;
Right was the pathway, leading to this.

We which are alive and remain unto the coming of the Lord shall not prevent (precede) them.   I Thess. 4:15

We have had days of sadness since they were called away, but oh, we're filled with gladness whene'er we think of them. We have had times of weeping as time has marched along, since we have left them sleeping, but ne'er a tear for them. We have had hours of praying, beset by want and care, but prayer has changed to praising, our tears were not for them. We have had deep repentings, for yielding to sin's power, but oh, they left off sinning in that eventful hour. We have seen Christ but dimly, by faith, and not by sight, but they have seen Him clearly in everlasting light.

> Yet soon WE shall be with THEM, and be
>   with Christ as they;
> Oh! let us not grow weary of waiting for
>   that day.

— Choice Gleanings

An old Chinese Christian died, and her family greeted the missionary with the words: "We are so sorry you are not in time to see her alive, but the King commanded her presence at 4 A.M., and of course, she gladly obeyed. We are all overcome with the honor." Instead of sorrow there was a hushed sense of awe in that poor home, and they only spoke of "her exceeding weight of glory." What a lesson for all Christian mourners!

> Why should our tears in sorrow flow?
>   The King recalls His own,
> And bids them leave a world of woe for
>   an immortal crown.

— Choice Gleanings

The coming of the Lord draweth nigh.   James 5:8

When he came . . . he found nothing but leaves.   Mark 11:13

Out of this world I shall never take things of gold and silver I make.
All that I cherish and hoard away, after I leave, on this earth must stay.
Though I have toiled for a painting rare to hang on the wall, I must leave it there;
Though I call it mine, and boast its worth, I must give it up when I leave this earth.
All that I gather and all that I keep I must leave behind when I fall asleep;
And I often wonder what I shall own in that other life when I pass alone.
Shall the great Judge find when my task is through that my spirit has gathered some riches too?
Or shall at last be it mine to find that all I worked for I left behind?

Ah, who shall thus the Master meet,
And bring but withered leaves?
Ah, who shall at the Savior's feet,
When found at His own judgment seat,
Lay down for golden sheaves—Nothing but leaves?

—*Choice Gleanings*

He sojourned in the land . . . he looked for a city. Heb. 11:9, 10

He looked for a city and lived in a tent . . . A pilgrim to glory right onward he went . . . God's promise his solace, so royal his birth . . . No wonder he sought not the glories of earth.

He looked for a city his God should prepare . . . No mansion on earth could he covet or share . . . For had not God told him that royal abode . . . Awaited His coming on ending the road.

He looked for a city; if sometimes he sighed . . . To be trudging the road, all earth's glory denied . . . The thought of that city changed sighing to song . . . For the road might be rough but it could not be long.

He looked for a city; his hope, Lord, we share . . . And know that bright city, which Thou dost prepare . . . We'll dwell in forever, since willing to be . . . Just pilgrims with Jesus, our roof a tent-tree.

Home! Home! Sweet, Sweet Home! A Welcome from Jesus awaits us at Home.

— Choice Gleanings

HOME

A HOUSE is built of logs and stones,
Of tiles and posts and tiers;
A HOME is built of loving deeds
That stand a thousand years.

A Christian home is earth's sweetest picture of heaven.

One of the most important pieces of furniture for the home is the family altar.

A little girl, who was asked where her home was, said, "Where mother is."

A stranger is one away from home, but a pilgrim is on his way home.

Home is the place where we are treated best and grumble most.

The first indication of domestic happiness is the love of one's home.

If your house is merely a place to eat and sleep, it ceases to be home.

Many American homes nowadays seem to be on three shifts. Father is on the night shift, mother is on the day shift, and the children shift for themselves.

A broken home is the world's greatest wreck.

An old-timer is one who remembers when a babysitter was called Mother.

Many modern homes are merely filling stations.

HOME, SWEET HOME

When each lives
For the other
And all live
FOR GOD.

HOME—a world of strife shut out, a world of love shut in.

HOME— a place where the small are great, and the great are small.

HOME— the father's kingdom, the mother's world, and the children's paradise.

HOME— where we grumble the most, and are treated the best.

HOME— the center of our affection, round which our heart's best wishes twine.

HOME— the place where our stomachs get three square meals a day and our hearts a thousand.

—Charles M. Crowe

A house is built by human hands . . .
but a home is built by human hearts.

He is happiest, be he king or peasant,
who finds peace in his home.

Children need
MODELS
rather than
CRITICS.

Woe to the house
where the
HEN
crows louder
than the
ROOSTER

Quiet evening,
Blissful hour,
Work is done,
Shadows lower.
Night is nigh,
Sweet repose,
Thoughts ascend,
To God who knows.

HONESTY

Honesty is the thing that keeps you from turning to the end of the book to see how the story ends.

Then, again, perhaps honesty is the best policy because it has so little competition.

It takes an honest man to tell whether he's tired or just lazy.

HONESTY PAYS,
but it doesn't seem to pay enough
to suit some people.
Frank H. Hubbard

An honest man is the noblest work of God.

—Alexander Pope

You cannot lift your children to a
higher level than that on which
you live yourself.

HUMILITY

You should ask God for
HUMILITY,
but never thank Him that
you've attained it.

When you know you've got humility,
you've lost it.

The greatest truths are the simplest;
so are men and women.

In the Christian life we must lose to gain; we must give to
obtain; we must be humble to be exalted; we must be least to be
greatest; we must die to live.

The beginning of greatness is to be little,
the increase of greatness is to be less,
and the perfection of greatness is to be nothing.

Humility is the first of virtues—
for other people.

Oliver Wendell Holmes

God giveth grace to the humble. When we try to avoid being humbled, we are avoiding a means of grace.

We wouldn't worry so much
about what other people thought of us if
we knew how seldom they did.

He is made more worthy
who dispenses
with what he deserves

INCONSISTENCY

BIRD-LIKE TRUST

Said the robin to the sparrow,
  "I would surely like to know
Why these anxious human beings
  Fret about and worry so!"
Said the sparrow to the robin,
  "I imagine it must be
That they have no heavenly Father
Such as cares for you and me!"

Some people are making such thorough preparations for rainy days that they aren't able to enjoy today's sunshine.	He that cannot forgive others breaks the bridge over which he must pass; for every man has a need to be forgiven.
As snow in summer, and as rain in harvest, so honour is not seemly for a fool (Prov. 26:1).	A jewel of gold in a swine's snout, so is a fair lady without discretion (Prov. 11:22).
The hardest job for youngsters is to learn good manners without seeing an example in their own parents.	It seems incredible — 35,000,000 laws on our books and not one single improvement on the Ten Commandments.

Why is it that most people want The FRONT seat in the bus, The BACK seat in church and The MIDDLE of the road?

IT IS SAID our great-grandfathers called it the holy Sabbath, our grandfathers the Sabbath, our fathers Sunday, and we call it the weekend. We have substituted the holiday for the holy day, recreation for reverence, games for godliness, and dissipation for devotion. In short, we use the gift of the Lord's Day to destroy the (its) Giver.

The Alliance Witness

**Everything is
WRONG
that is
ALMOST RIGHT.**

Half-heartedness consists of Serving God in such a way as Not to offend the devil.

The man who makes a mistake and doesn't correct it is making another mistake.	If a man cannot look you in the eye, there is something wrong with his view of life.
When you corner an opposum, he plays dead; when you corner a hypocrite, he plays alive.	This fast age seems more concerned about speed than direction.
He that is greedy of gain troubleth his own house; but he that hateth gifts shall live (Prov. 15:27).	Too often the Christmas bells with the merriest jingle are the ones on the cash register.

America is the only country where they lock up the jury and let the prisoners go home.

One of the troubles in the world today is the fact that we have allowed the Golden Rule to become a bit tarnished.

—Martin Vanbee

Humility is a strange thing: the moment you think you have it, you've lost it.

It is impossible to be rightly governed without God and the Bible.

There is a way that seemeth right unto a man, but the end thereof are the ways of death (Prov. 16:25).

**People do
ODD
things
to get
EVEN.**

People who get something for nothing often kick about the quality.

It is wrong for a person to profess what he does not possess.

Our walk must square with our talk.

A lot of trouble in this world is caused by combining a NARROW mind with a WIDE mouth.

Some people are like blotters—they soak up everything but get it backwards.

Those who say
they will forgive,
but can't forget
the injury
simply bury the hatchet
while they leave
the handle uncovered
for immediate use.

It is hard to express love with a clenched fist.

A rocking horse makes motion, but no progress.

It is hard to pay for bread that has been eaten.

Beware of a rubber conscience and a concrete heart.

**Those who stand for nothing
are apt to fall for anything.**

When your outgo exceeds your income,
your upkeep is your downfall.

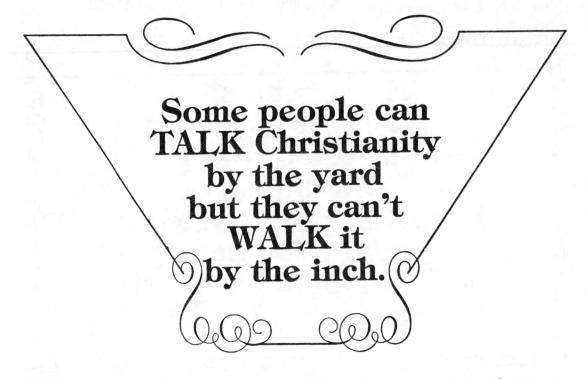

Some people can
TALK Christianity
by the yard
but they can't
WALK it
by the inch.

Men are known by the way they
TALK
WALK
BALK.

The angels from their home on high
Look down to earth with pitying eye,
That where we are passing guests,
We build such strong and solid nests;
Yet where we hope to live for aye,
We scarce take heed one stone to lay.

KINDNESS

Put on therefore . . . mercies, kindness, humbleness of mind, meekness, longsuffering. Col. 3:12

Kindness is love doing little things, things that seem scarcely worth doing, and yet which mean much to those for whom they are wrought. Kindness lends a hand when another is burdened. It speaks the cheerful word when a heart is discouraged. It gives a cup of cold water when one is thirsty. It is always doing good turns to somebody. It goes about performing little ministries with a touch of blessing. It scatters its favors everywhere. Few qualities do more to make a life bright and beautiful! Lord, make me kind today, full of love!

> Scatter then your seeds of kindness, all enriching as you go —
> Leave them. Trust the Harvest Giver; He will make each seed to grow.
> So until the happy end, your life shall never lack a friend.

> — Choice Gleanings

Kindness is the language that the deaf can hear and the dumb can understand.

Wherever there is a human being there is an opportunity for kindness.

Kindness is the controlling spring which holds back the slamming door.

The ones whom you should try to get even with are the ones who have helped you.

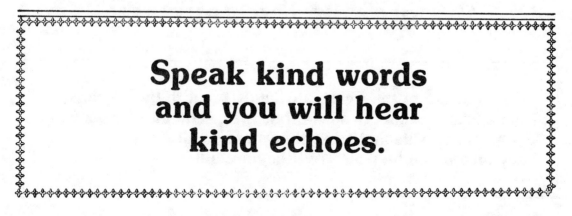

Speak kind words and you will hear kind echoes.

Let me be a little kinder, let me be a little blinder
To the faults of those about me; let me praise a little more.
Let me be a little meeker with the brother that is weaker;
Let me think more of my neighbor and a little less of me.

'Twas her thinking of others
made you think of her.

Kind HEARTS are the GARDENS,
Kind THOUGHTS are the ROOTS,
Kind WORDS are the FLOWERS,
Kind DEEDS are the FRUITS.

Let us be the first to
show a friendly sign,
to nod first,
smile first,
speak first,
and—if such a thing is necessary—
to forgive first.

The only way on earth to
multiply happiness
is to divide it.

The secret of happy living
is not to do what you like
but to like what you do.

The greater the man, the greater the courtesy.

An arm of aid to the weak, a friendly hand to the helpless,
Kind words so short to speak, but their echo may be endless;
The world is wide and these things are small
They may be nothing . . . but they are all.

It was only a glad, "GOOD MORNING!"
As she passed along the way
But it spread the morning's glory
Over the livelong day.

When it comes to helping others,
some people stop at nothing.

 How seldom we weigh our neighbor
in the same balance with ourselves.

He most lives who lives for others.

Then deem it not an idle thing
A pleasant word to speak;
The face you wear, the thought you bring
A heart may heal or break.

— J. G. Whittier

Kindness is like snow—
it beautifies everything
it covers.

KNOWLEDGE

It is better to know less
than to know a lot that
isn't so.

The learning and knowledge that we have is at the most but little compared with that of which we are ignorant. — Plato	The fear of the Lord is the beginning of knowledge (Prov. 1:7).
	He who will not learn from anyone except himself has a fool for a teacher.
The wisest man is the man that has made up his mind to be "a fool for Christ's sake."	Consciousness of ignorance is no small part of knowledge.

KNOWLEDGE
humbleth a great man,
astonishes a common man,
puffs up a little man.

Education cannot cure sin;
it only sharpens sin's tools.

A wise man is like a pin;
his head keeps him from going too far.

LIGHTER VEIN

When was the last time you said somebody didn't know beans about something, or described a fog as being thick as pea soup, or called a political speech a lot of applesauce?

It probably wasn't very long ago, because we Americans really take the cake when it comes to using foods in our everyday figures of speech. For example, when things go right, they are in apple pie order, and life is a bowl of cherries. But when they go wrong, it's a fine kettle of fish, or a pretty pickle.

If a man is important, he's top banana. If he's not, he may be just a meatball. If he's clumsy, he's butterfingered. If he's cowardly, he's chicken-livered. If he's poised, he's cool as a cucumber. If he's smart, he's an egghead. And if he's a prizefighter, he very likely has cauliflower ears. If he talks too much, he spills the beans. And if he doesn't talk enough, he clams up.

Moreover, he doesn't earn money, he earns dough, or he brings home the bacon. And if he's working for peanuts, his wife may egg him on to butter up the boss.

If something is good, it's a peach. If it's bad, it's a lemon. And that may lead to a rhubarb. But someone will say it's just sour grapes.

You may think you deserve an egg in your beer, but if you're not worth your salt, you may wind up eating humble pie. . . and that would be getting your just desserts.

Finally, a pretty girl is a tomato, or quite a dish, and the boys may want to spoon with her. But if one asks her to elope, she may say she "cantaloupe."

And now, just to ice the cake, I want to say that you may take most claims with a grain of salt.

Distance lends enchantment, but not when you're out of gas.	Flattery is soft soap—and soft soap is 95 percent lye.
Some people have only three occasions for attending church: when they are hatched, matched, and dispatched.	A black cat following you is bad luck, depending on whether you are a man or a mouse.

Men are known by the way they
    TALK
      WALK
        BALK.
	When a man won't listen to his conscience, it's usually because he doesn't want advice from a total stranger.

Some husbands know all the answers because they have been listening for years.	Some folks would rather blow their own horn than listen to Sousa's band.
You would get cheated if you gave a penny for some people's thoughts.	**With a small boy, cleanliness is not next to godliness, it's next to impossible.**
A lot of folks who never took music lessons are good at fiddling around.	Face powder may catch a man, but it takes baking powder to hold him.
CHEER UP! Birds also have bills, but they keep on singing.	Money may talk but today's dollar doesn't have much to say.

Let a pig and a boy
have everything they want,
and you'll get a good pig and a bad boy.

The most powerful KING on earth is Wor-KING;
The laziest KING on earth is Shir-KING;
One of the worst KINGS is Smo-KING;
The wittiest KING on earth is Jo-KING;
The quietest KING on earth is Thin-KING;
The thirstiest KING is Drin-KING;
The slyest KING is Win-KING;
And the noisiest KING is Tal-KING.

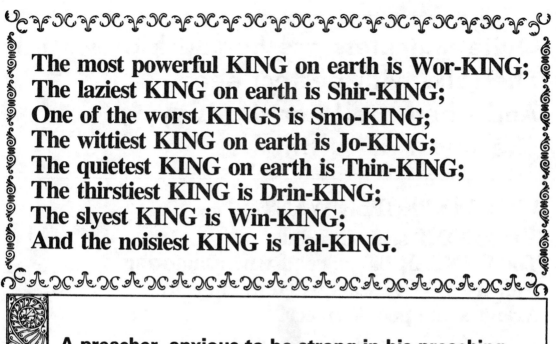

A preacher, anxious to be strong in his preaching without offending anyone, said something like this:
"If you don't repent, as it were;
and be converted, in a measure;
you will go to hell, to a certain extent.

Those of you
WHO THINK YOU KNOW IT ALL
are very annoying
TO THOSE OF US WHO DO.

It's the LITTLE THINGS that bother us,
And keep us on the rack;
We can sit upon a MOUNTAIN,
But not on a TACK.

Quite matchless are her dark brown iiii,
She talks with perfect eeee,
And when I tell her she is yyyy,
She says I am a tttt.

WHY DO PEOPLE WANT—
The FRONT seats in a bus,
The CENTER of the road when motoring,
And the BACK seats when in church?
Aren't some people queer?

A middle-aged woman is one
who is too young for MEDICARE
and too old for MEN TO CARE.

As a rule a man is a fool,
When it's HOT he wants it COOL,
When it's COOL he wants it HOT,
Always wants what is not.

One danger of overeating—it may cause you to live beyond your seams.

Even a tombstone will say good things about a fellow when he is down.

Sooner or later, a man reaches his "B" period:

ifocals
aldness
ridgework
ulge

About the only thing that comes to the man who waits is WHISKERS.

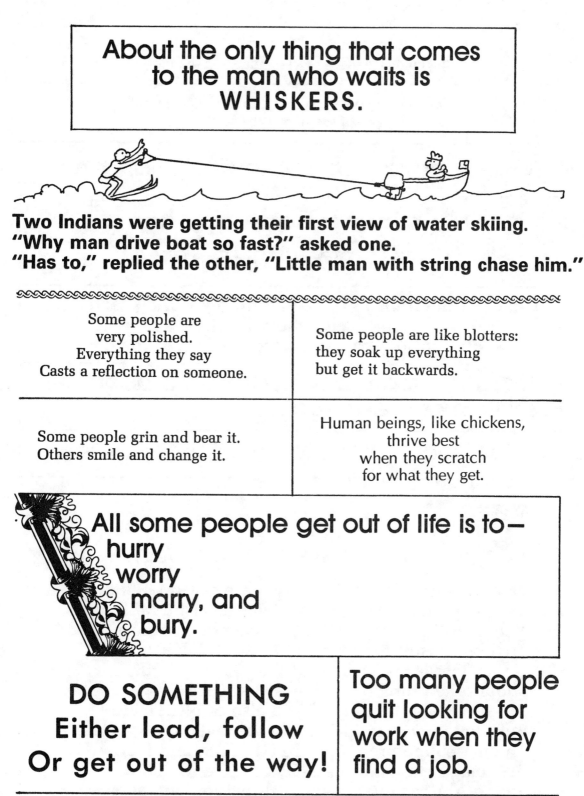

**Two Indians were getting their first view of water skiing.
"Why man drive boat so fast?" asked one.
"Has to," replied the other, "Little man with string chase him."**

Some people are
very polished.
Everything they say
Casts a reflection on someone.

Some people are like blotters:
they soak up everything
but get it backwards.

Some people grin and bear it.
Others smile and change it.

Human beings, like chickens,
thrive best
when they scratch
for what they get.

All some people get out of life is to—
hurry
worry
marry, and
bury.

DO SOMETHING
Either lead, follow
Or get out of the way!

Too many people
quit looking for
work when they
find a job.

People who look down on their neighbors are usually living on a bluff.

Don't criticize your wife's judgment— see whom she married.	'Tis not the hen that cackles most that lays the most eggs.

For safe driving—see that all the nuts are tight, except the one at the wheel.

Only a baker can make dough and loaf.

My mind is made up, don't confuse me with the facts!

The chief difference between a gum-chewing teen-ager and a cud-chewing cow is the thoughtful expression on the face of the cow.

There are too many hydromatic people— shiftless and easy-going.

Spit, spat, and spite are close relatives.

UR FUNNY AMERICAN LANGUAGE

One fowl is a GOOSE, but two are called GEESE,
Yet the plural of MOOSE should never be MEESE.
You may find a lone MOUSE or a whole nest of MICE,
Then why isn't the plural of HOUSE HICE?
If the singular is THIS, and the plural is THESE,
Should the plural of KISS ever be KEESE?
We speak of a BROTHER and also of BRETHERN,
But though we say MOTHER we never say METHERN.
The masculine pronouns are HE, HIS, and HIM,
But imagine a feminine SHE, SHIS, and SHIM.
So the American language, I think you will agree,
Is the funniest language we ever did see.

LIVING

AUTUMN'S HERE

The summer sun
Has lost its heat.
The autumn wind
Has cooled the earth.
Green trees shiver,
Their leaves turn brown.
The sky darkens
And cries at times.
Dry riverbeds
Come back to life.
White clouds of fog
Blanket the ground.
Sweaters and coats
Are worn again.
Outside, you miss
The warmth of home.
People hurry along,
Their breath is mist.
Days are shorter;
Nights are long.
Fires burn high
And embers glow.
Life still goes on;
Summer is missed.

—Eugene Grijalva

We get the sweetest comfort
When we wear the oldest shoe;
We love the old friends better
Than we'll ever love the new.
Old songs are more appealing
To the wearied heart—and so
We find the sweetest music
In the tunes of long ago.
There's a kind of mellow sweetness
In a thing growing old.
Each year that rolls around it
Leaves an added touch of gold.

Tomorrow is not promised us,
So let us take today,
And make the most of it,
The once we pass this way.
Just speak aloud the kindly thought,
And do the kindly deed;
And try and see and understand
Some fellow creature's need.
Tomorrow is not promised us,
Nor any other day.
So let us make the most of it,
The once we pass this way.

— Louise Mae Hagan

When as a CHILD I laughed and slept—TIME CREPT.
When as a YOUTH I dreamt and talked—TIME WALKED.
When I became a FULL-GROWN man—TIME RAN.
When OLDER still I daily grew—TIME FLEW.
Soon I shall find in TRAVELING ON—TIME IS GONE.
O, Christ, to behold Thy beauty THEN.

LIFE

Man's life means:
Tender teens
Teachable twenties
Tireless thirties
Fiery forties
Forceful fifties
Serious sixties
Sacred seventies
Aching eighties
Shortening breath
Death
The sod
GOD!

LET US TAKE TIME

To give God worship, service, and communion.
To live with our friends while we have them. A coffin is
a poor place for the warm handclasp and the cheery
greeting. To forgive our enemies. Jesus found time to
do it between the blows of the hammer. To go slower
up hill when we are young, and down hill when we are
old.

Live each day as if it were your last—
it could be!

I live to die,
I die to live;
the more I die,
the more I live.

The truest end of life
is to know the life
that will never end.

Little drops of water, little grains of sand,
Make the mighty ocean and the pleasant land.
So the little moments, humble though they be,
Make the mighty ages of eternity.

— Julia Carney

LIFE IS TOO SHORT

To remember slights and insults.
To cherish grudges that rob me of happiness.
To waste time in doing things that are of no value.
To give my youth to the devil and my old age to God.

LIFE IS TOO LONG

To be unprepared for its eternal glory.
To act as though death closed the account instead
of opening it.

IT DOES NOT PAY

To "have a good time" at the expense of an
uneasy conscience the next morning.
To lose one's temper at the expense of losing a
friend.
To give God the husks instead of the heart.
To live at all unless we live for all.

The best way to live in the world is to live above it.

Some people know how to make a living
but don't know how to live.

The secret of life is not to do what one likes,
but to try to like what one has to do.

—Dinah Muloch Craik

It is not how long you live
but for what you live
that counts.

It is better to make a good life than a good living.

LOVE

FAITH - Makes all things possible.
HOPE - Makes all things bright.
LOVE - Makes all things easy.

Better a dinner of herbs where love is, than a stalled ox and hatred thereby (Prov. 15:17).	The glory of life is love, not to be loved; to give, not to get; to serve, not to be served.
Money will buy a fine dog, but only love will make him wag his tail.	It is never loving that empties the heart, nor giving that empties the purse.
If slighted, slight the slight, and love the slighter.	Charity (love) begins at home — but it does not stay there.
Love looks through a telescope; envy through a microscope.	The sunlight of love will kill all the germs of jealousy and hate.
Law makes us act from outward compulsion, but love makes us serve from inward compassion.	A "bit of love" is the only bit that will put a bridle on the tongue. — Beck
"Tis better to have loved and lost Than never to have loved at all. — Tennyson	Love is like the measles — worse when it comes late in life.

Love sent my Lord to the cross of shame,
Love found a way, O praise His holy name!

Works, and not words, are the proof of love.

Love is its own reward; hate is its own punishment.

There is more pleasure in loving than in being loved.

Duty makes us do things well, but love makes us do them beautifully.

The glory of life is to love not to be loved; to give not to get; to serve, not to be served.

It is natural to love them that love us, but it is supernatural to love them that hate us.

Love saw the guilt of sin, and sought a basis of pardon.
Love saw the alienation of sin, and sought a ground of reconciliation.
Love saw the defilement of sin, and sought a way of cleansing.
Love saw the depravity of sin, and sought a means of restoration.
Love saw the enslavement of sin, and sought an instrument of emancipation.
Love saw the malady of sin, and sought a balm of healing.
Love saw the condemnation of sin, and sought a method of justification.
Love saw the death of sin, and sought a way of life.
Love sought, and love found.

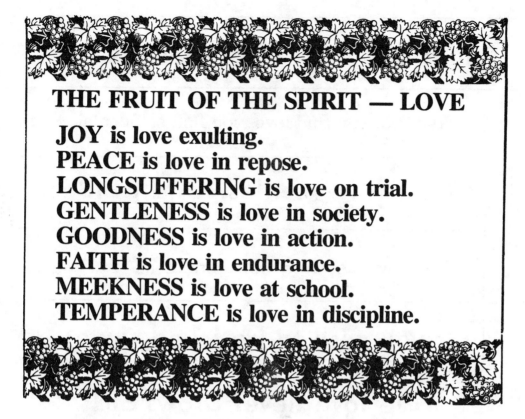

THE FRUIT OF THE SPIRIT — LOVE

JOY is love exulting.
PEACE is love in repose.
LONGSUFFERING is love on trial.
GENTLENESS is love in society.
GOODNESS is love in action.
FAITH is love in endurance.
MEEKNESS is love at school.
TEMPERANCE is love in discipline.

We like someone BECAUSE.
We love someone ALTHOUGH.

Those who deserve love the least need it the most.

It is hard to express love with a clenched fist.

The love of heaven makes a man heavenly.

If you give love, you will have love.

I like not only to be loved, but to be told that I am loved; the realm of silence is large enough beyond the grave.

– George Elliot

Faults are thick where love is thin.

Wherever you find love, you find self-denial.

Where love resides, God abides.

They love us truly who correct us freely.

If you wish to be loved, love!

True love never grows old.

PERFECT LOVE

Slow to suspect—quick to trust
Slow to condemn—quick to justify
Slow to offend—quick to defend
Slow to expose—quick to shield
Slow to reprimand—quick to forbear
Slow to belittle—quick to appreciate
Slow to demand—quick to give
Slow to provoke—quick to conciliate
Slow to hinder—quick to help
Slow to resent—quick to forgive

MAN

A man is like a piece of steel—he's no good when he loses his temper.

Man is the creation in whom God has decreed He shall be represented and glorified.

It doesn't take great men to do mighty things for God, just consecrated men.

The measure of a truly great man is the courtesy with which he treats a little man.

Find out what your temptations are, and you will find out largely what you are yourself.

It takes a strong man to hold his tongue.

As a general rule, a man is about as big as the things that make him mad.

Tell me with whom you associate, and I will tell you who you are.

A man wrapped up in himself makes a very small package.

The fear of God can deliver from the fear of man.

If you think God's thoughts, you'll never think highly of yourself.

You can tell how big a man is by observing how much it takes to discourage him.

Great men never feel great. Small men never feel small.

MARRIAGE

ADVICE TO THE WIFE:
Be to his virtues very kind.
Be to his faults a little blind.

Marriage used to be a contract. Now many regard it as a ninety-day option.

Whoso findeth a wife findeth a good thing, and obtaineth favor the Lord (Prov. 18:22).

Let every husband stay a true lover, and every wife remain a sweetheart too.

Who gains a good son-in-law, gains a good son; who finds a bad one, loses his daughter.

Love is like the measles—worse when it comes late in life.

Never be yoked to one who refuses the yoke of Christ.

June is the month when girls look at the BRIDE side of life.

A woman worries about the future until she gets a husband, while a man never worries about the future until he gets a wife.

Many a man in love with a dimple has made the mistake of marrying the whole girl.

Man's best possession is a sympathetic wife.

Some say
SINGLENESS IS BLISS
and
MARRIAGE IS A BLISTER.

BLESSINGS FOR THE MARRIED

Blessed are the husband and wife who continue to be affectionate, considerate and loving after the wedding bells have ceased ringing.

Blessed are the husband and wife who are as polite and courteous to one another as they are to their friends.

Blessed are they who have a sense of humor, for this attribute will be a handy shock absorber.

Blessed are the married couples who abstain from alcoholic beverages.

Blessed are they who love their mates more than any other person in the world, and who joyfully fulfill their marriage vow of a lifetime of fidelity and mutual helpfulness to each other.

Blessed are they who remember to thank God for their food before they partake of it, and who set aside some time each day for the reading of the Bible and prayer.

Blessed are they who attain parenthood, for children are a heritage of the Lord.

Blessed are those mates who never speak loudly to each other and who make their home a place "where seldom is heard a discouraging word."

Blessed are the husband and wife who faithfully attend the worship service of the church.

Blessed are the husband and wife who can work out their problems of adjustment without interference from relatives.

Blessed is the couple who have a complete understanding about financial matters and who have worked our perfect partnership with all the money under control of both.

Blessed are the husband and wife who humbly dedicate their lives and their home to Christ and practice the teachings of Christ in their home by being unselfish, loyal and loving.

The sea of matrimony is filled with hardships.

Before you run in double harness, look well to the horse.

The bonds of matrimony aren't worth much unless the interest is kept up.

Wedlock should be a padlock.

Never marry but for love; but see that thou lovest what is lovely.

Choose a wife by your ear rather than by your eye.

A smoking stove and a scolding wife soon drive a man out of doors.

A little house well fill'd, a little field well till'd, and a little wife well will'd, are great riches.

The average girl would rather have beauty than brains, because the average man can see better than he can think.

OBEDIENCE

Our great need is not MORE KNOWLEDGE,
but rather
to put INTO PRACTICE what we already know.

OBEDIENCE
is better than
SACRIFICE.

My Lord knows the way
through the wilderness.
All I have to do
is follow.

To know God's will
is life's greatest treasure.
To do God's will
is life's greatest pleasure.

It is a greater thing to obey the Word
of the Lord than to preach it.

OPTIMISM

The world looks brighter from behind a smile.

An optimist is
a man who thinks he can find
some big strawberries
in the bottom of the box.

Optimism is the determination
to see more in something
than there is.

An optimist sees
an opportunity in every calamity;
a pessimist sees
a calamity in every opportunity.

An optimist is
a man who can hand his car
over to a parking lot attendant
without looking back.

PARENTS

TO ALL PARENTS

"I'll lend you for a little time
A child of Mine," He said,
"For you to love the while he lives
And mourn for when he is dead.
It may be six or seven years,
Or twenty two or three;
But will you, 'til I call him back,
Take care of him for Me?
He'll bring his charms to gladden you,
And should his stay be brief,
You'll have his loving memories
As solace for your grief.

I cannot promise he will stay,
Since all from earth return,
But there are lessons taught down there
I want this child to learn,
I've looked the wide world over
In My search for teachers true,
And from all the throngs that crowd
Life's lanes I've selected you.
Now will you give him all your love,
Not think the labor vain,
Nor hate Me when I come to call
To take him back again?"

I fancied that I heard them say,
"Dear Lord, Thy will be done."
For all the joy Thy child shall bring,
The risk of grief we'll run.
We'll shelter him with tenderness,
We'll love him while we may.
And for the happiness we've known.
Forever grateful stay;
But should the angels call for him
Sooner than we've planned
We'll brave the bitter grief
That comes and try to understand."

—Edgar A. Guest

PATIENCE

True patience
means
waiting without worrying.

Patience is accepting a difficult situation
without giving God a deadline to remove it.

Patience
is the best remedy
for most trouble.

Don't force issues.
Learn to wait
and be patient.

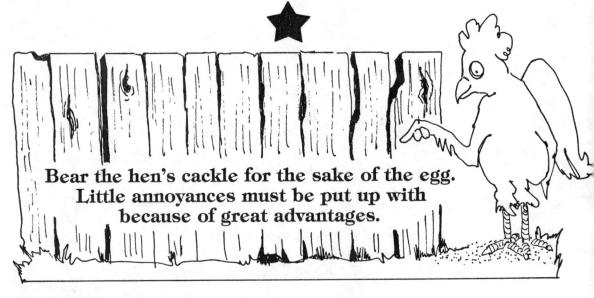

Bear the hen's cackle for the sake of the egg.
Little annoyances must be put up with
because of great advantages.

PLAIN TRUTH

Not what these hands have done
   Can save this guilty soul;
Not what this toiling flesh has borne,
   Can make my spirit whole.
Not what I feel or do
   Can give me peace with God;
Not all my prayers nor sighs nor tears,
   Can ease my awful load.
THY WORK alone, O Christ,
   Can ease this weight of sin;
THY BLOOD alone, O Lamb of God,
   Can give me peace within.
                — Horatius Bonar

Some minds are like concrete— thoroughly mixed and permanently set.

Christians wouldn't have to worry so much how their children turn out if they'd worry more about what time they turn in.

People look at us six days of a week to find out whether we really mean what we say and do on the seventh.

Every person has two ends:
    an end to think with
    and an end to sit with.
What he accomplishes
    depends on the end he chooses—
        heads, he wins
        tails, he loses.

It often happens that big men can be very petty about small things.

Chasing after pleasure Is a true confession of an UNSATISFIED life.

THE PSALMIST SAID: "In Thy presence is FULLNESS OF JOY; at Thy right hand are PLEASURES FOR EVERMORE." (Psalm 16:11)

When happiness gets into your system, it is bound to break out on the face.

Stones and sticks are thrown only at fruit-bearing trees.

If some people had an operation to remove their conscience, it would be a fairly simple operation.

If you have been born once, you will die twice; but if you have been born twice, you will die but once.

The greater thing in this world is not so much where we stand, as in what direction we are going.

There is no good in arguing with the inevitable. The only argument available with an east wind is to put on your overcoat.

You are not just ONE PERSON, but THREE—the one YOU think you are, the one OTHER PEOPLE think you are, and the person YOU REALLY ARE.

Just about the time you think you can make both ends meet, somebody moves the ends.

When a man begins to amass wealth, it is a question whether God is going to gain a fortune or lose a man.

Truth doesn't hurt unless it ought to.

Blessed is he who has learned to admire but not envy, to follow but not imitate, to praise but not flatter, and to lead but not manipulate.

When you brood over your troubles, you hatch despair.

Every man must live with the man he makes of himself.

Folks with a lot of brass are seldom polished.

Too many people mistake Easter Day for Decoration Day.

When you get all wrinkled with care and worry, it's time you have your faith lifted.

The thing that makes men and rivers crooked is following the lines of least resistance.

No man is free who is not master of himself.

Discussion is an evidence of knowledge. Argument is an evidence of ignorance.

Nothing is settled until it is settled right.

It's bad to have an empty purse, But an empty head is a whole lot worse.

A man who rows a boat doesn't have time to rock it.

D. L. Moody once said: "A holy life will make the deepest impression. Lighthouses blow no horns: they just shine."

TRUTH

Great truths are not caught on the fly.

Blessed are the hard-of-hearing for they miss much small talk.

He never rises high who does not know how to pray.

PRAISE

We will praise Him
   for all that is past,
and trust Him
   for all that is to come.

Praising God for blessings
extends them.
Praising God for troubles
ends them.

He who merits praise he never receives
is better off than
he who receives praise he never merits.

Hem your blessings with praise
lest they unravel.

PRAYER

I started early with my chores,
But even so I started wrong.
My labor yielded me no gain—
I should have started with a song.

I battled time this trying day
To find my efforts were a loss;
I had to leave some plans undone—
Tasks multiplied and I grew cross.

Tonight I ponder while I rest—
All day I fought rebellious tares.
Yet that has always been my lot
When days do not begin with prayer.

True prayer is a way of life, not just a case of emergency.	Prayer will make a man cease from sin, or sin will entice a man to cease from prayer.
Many prayers go to the dead letter office of heaven for want of sufficient direction.	Strength in prayer is better than length in prayer.
No day is well spent without communication with God.	When thou prayest, rather let thy heart be without words than thy words without heart.

Prayer without work is beggary; Work without prayer is slavery.

A PRAYER OF THE AGED

"Father, Thou knowest I am growing old. Keep me from becoming talkative and possessed with the idea that I must express myself on every subject. Release me from the craving to straighten out everyone's affairs.

"Keep my mind free from the recital of endless detail. Give me wings to go to the point. Seal my lips when I am inclined to tell of my aches and pains . . . teach me the glorious lesson that occasionally I may be wrong . . . make me thoughtful but not nosy, helpful but not bossy. With my vast store of wisdom and experience it does seem a pity not to use it all, but Thou knowest, Lord, that I want a few friends in the end. AMEN!"

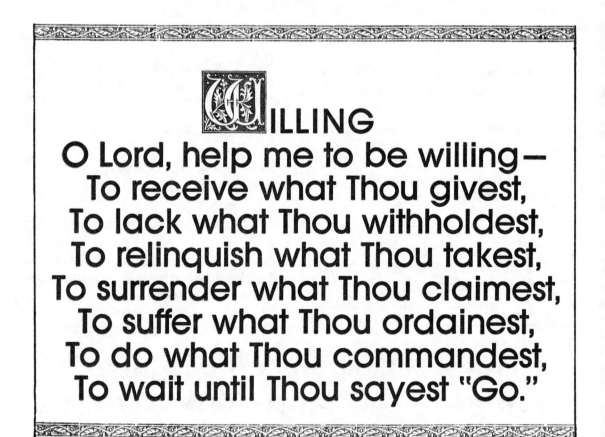

WILLING
O Lord, help me to be willing—
To receive what Thou givest,
To lack what Thou withholdest,
To relinquish what Thou takest,
To surrender what Thou claimest,
To suffer what Thou ordainest,
To do what Thou commandest,
To wait until Thou sayest "Go."

PRAYER

The Lord always hears our prayers,
But He does not always say, "Yes!"
Sometimes He says, "Wait"
Sometimes He says, "No"
For He has something better for us.

God's delays are not denials,
He has heard your prayer;
He knows all about your trials,
Knows your every care.

God's delays are not denials,
Help is on the way,
He is watching o'er life's dials,
Bringing forth that day.

God's delays are not denials,
You will find Him true,
Working through the darkest trials,
What is best for you.

When God does not immediately respond to the cries of His children, it is because He wants to accomplish some gracious purpose in their lives. If you are waiting for an answer of some heartfelt petition, don't become impatient. Commit the matter into the hands of your loving heavenly Father and trust His wisdom.

Don't pray unless you believe God will answer.

The best way to remember people is in prayer.

"Praying ALWAYS. . . ."
Eph. 6:18
"CONTINUE in prayer. . . ."
Col. 4:2
"Pray WITHOUT CEASING."
I Thess. 5:17
". . . Continuing STEADFASTLY in prayer."
Rom. 12:12

I do not always bend the knee to pray;
  I often pray in crowded city street
In some hard crisis of a busy day—
  Prayer is my sure and comforting retreat.
Here at my office desk I ask His aid,
  No matter where I am I crave His care;
In moments when my soul is sore afraid
  It comforts most to know He's everywhere.

"The prayer power," says J. Hudson Taylor "has never been tried to its full capacity . . . If we want to see mighty wonders of divine power and grace wrought in the place of weakness, failure and disappointment, let us answer God's standing challenge, "Call unto me, and I will answer thee, and show thee great and mighty things which thou knowest not!"

I sat and gazed in silence
At the azure sky overhead.
In the glory of that moment,
A simple prayer was said.
I thanked God for all the grandeur,
For His beauty everywhere,
I praised the Great Creator
As I sat in silent prayer.
I found an inspiration
And a peace within my soul,
I took the time to worship
And I felt myself made whole.

— Lois Anne Williams

MY PRAYER

Teach me, Lord, to keep sweet and gentle in all the events of life, in disappointments, in thoughtlessness of others, in the insincerity of those I trusted, in the unfaithfulness of those on whom I relied.

Help me to put myself aside, to think of the happiness of others, to hide my little pains and heartaches, so that I may be the only one to suffer from them.

Teach me to profit by the suffering that comes to me. Help me to use it that it may mellow me, not harden or embitter me; that it may make me broad in my forgiveness; kindly, sympathetic, and helpful.

More things are wrought by prayer than the world dreams of.	Arguments never settle things, but prayer changes things.
Life's best outlook is a prayerful uplook.	Embark upon no enterprise you cannot submit to the test of prayer.
Nothing lies beyond the reach of prayer except that which lies beyond the will of God.	The sacrifice of the wicked is an abomination to the Lord: but the prayer of the upright is his delight.
If I could hear Christ praying for me in the next room, I would not fear a million enemies. Yet distance makes no difference. He is praying for me. — Robert Murray McCheyne	Our business in prayer is, not to prescribe but to subscribe to the wisdom and will of God; to refer our case to Him, and then leave it with Him.

If trouble drives you to prayer,
prayer will drive the trouble away.

DEEP LIVING

We love to spread our branches;
  The root-life we neglect.
We love to shine in public,
  And human praise expect;
While in the inner chamber,
  Where creature voices cease,
We may meet God in silence,
  And breathe in Heaven's peace.

The secret of deep living
  Lies in the secret place
Where, time and sense forgotten,
  We see God face to face;
Beyond mere forms and symbols,
  Beyond mere words and signs,
Where in that hidden temple
  The light eternal shines.

—Max I. Reich

If you are a stranger to prayer,
you are a stranger to power.

Do not face the day until you have faced God.

Without prayer no work is well done.

God's answers are wiser than our prayers.

Prayer is hardest when it is hardest to pray.

Daily prayers lessen daily cares.

He stands best who kneels most.

Change matters of care to matters of prayer.

Prayerless pews make powerless pulpits.

Prayer is profitable whenever it is practiced.

Unanswered yet! Nay, do not say UNGRANTED;
perhaps your part is not yet fully done.
The work began when first your prayer was uttered,
and God will finish what He has begun.
If you keep faith's incense burning there,
His glory you will see—sometime—somewhere!

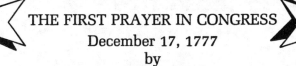

THE FIRST PRAYER IN CONGRESS
December 17, 1777
by
Rev. J. Duche, Chaplain

O Lord, our heavenly Father, High and Mighty, King of Kings and Lord of Lords, who dost from the Throne behold all the dwellers on earth and reignest with power supreme and uncontrolled over all kingdoms, empires and governments; look down in mercy we beseech Thee on these American States, who have fled to Thee from the rod of the oppressor, and thrown themselves on Thy gracious protection desiring henceforth to be dependent only on Thee. To Thee they have appealed for the righteousness of their cause. To Thee do they look up for that countenance and support which Thou alone canst give. Take them therefore Heavenly Father under Thy nurturing care. Give them wisdom in counsel and valor in the field. Defeat the malicious designs of our cruel adversaries. Convince them of the unrighteousness of their cause, and if they persist in their sanguinary purpose, O let the voice of thine own unerring justice, sounding in their hearts, constrain them to drop their weapons of war from their unnerved hands in the day of battle.

Be Thou present, O God of wisdom and direct the counsels of this honorable Assembly. Enable them to settle things on the best and surest foundation; that the scent of blood may speedily be closed, that order, harmony and peace may be effectually restored, and truth and justice and religion and piety may prevail and flourish among Thy people. Preserve the health of their bodies, and the vigor of their minds; shower down on them and the millions they represent such temporal blessings as Thou seest expedient for them in this world, and crown them with everlasting glory in the world to come. All this we ask in the name of and through the merits of Jesus Christ, Thy Son, our Savior. Amen.

For prayer without the heart,
the Lord will never hear;
Nor will He to those lips
attend whose prayers are
not sincere.

Do you mean God to
take you at your
word when you
pray?

Prayerlessness
begets
carelessness.

When we depend on man, we get what man can do;
when we depend on prayer, we get what God can do.

A praying
man can never
be a useless man.

There are three
answers to prayer:
YES
NO
WAIT AWHILE.

Prayer is a shield to the soul,
a delight to God,
and a scourge to Satan.

—Bunyan

A missionary and his helpers were forced to camp on a hill. They carried money and were fearful of an attack. After prayer, they went to sleep. Months later a brigand chief was brought to the mission hospital. He asked the missionary if he had soldiers to guard him that special night. "We intended to rob you," he said, "but we were afraid of the 27 soldiers." When the story was told in the homeland, someone said, "We had a prayer meeting that night, and there were just 27 of us present."

Yes, we are always wondering, wondering how—
Because we do not see
Someone—perhaps unknown and far away —
On bended knee.

— Choice Gleanings

"LORD, help me to be—
Intensely spiritual,
Perfectly natural,
Thoroughly practical."

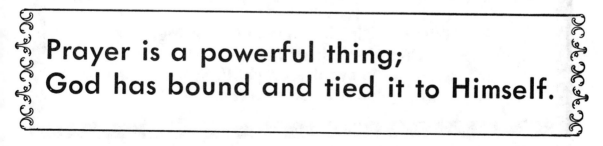

Prayer is a powerful thing;
God has bound and tied it to Himself.

In praying we must not forget that our prayers are to be answered. Some are answered just as we wish; some are answered in a way different from what we wish — in a better way! Some are answered by a change in us; some by a change in others. Some are answered by the giving of a greater strength to bear trials, and some by the lifting of the trials. Some at once; some in years to come; and some await eternity.

> I know not if the blessing sought
> Will come in just the way I thought,
> But leave my prayer with Him alone
> Whose will is wiser than my own,
> Assured that He will grant my quest
> Or send some answer far more blessed.
>
> —Choice Gleanings

> **Pray on! Pray on! Cease not to pray,**
> **And should the answer tarry, WAIT!**
> **Thy God will come, will surely come,**
> **And He can never come too late.**

To look around is to be distressed.
To look within is to be depressed.
To look up is to be blessed.

Satan trembles when he sees
the weakest Christian
on his knees.

> **When the Spirit prompts the asking,**
> **When the waiting heart believes,**
> **Then we know of each petition,**
> **Everyone who asks receives.**

LORD, make me a channel of Thy peace
That where there is hatred, I may bring love,
That where there is wrong, I may bring the spirit of forgiveness.
That where there is discord, I may bring harmony,
That where there is error, I may bring truth,
That where there is doubt, I may bring faith,
That where there is despair, I may bring hope,
That where there are shadows, I may bring light,
That where there is sadness, I may bring joy.

Lord, grant that I may seek rather
To comfort—than to be comforted;
To understand—than to be understood;
To love—than to be loved;
For it is by giving that one receives;
It is by self-forgetting that one finds;
It is by forgiving that one is forgiven;
It is by dying that one awakens to eternal life.

—St. Francis of Assisi

Last night my little boy confessed to me
Some childish wrong, And kneeling at my
knees he prayed: "Dear God, make me a man,
Like Daddy, wise and strong, I know You can!"

Then when he slept, I knelt beside his bed
confessed my sins, and with low bowed head I prayed:
"Oh, God, make me a child like my child here,
Pure, guileless, trusting Thee with faith sincere.'

"The one concern of the devil is to keep Christians from praying. He fears nothing from prayerless studies, prayerless work, prayerless religion. He laughs at our toil, mocks at our wisdom, but trembles when we pray."

Pray as though no work could help, and work as though prayer could not help.

Don't pray for tasks suited to your capacity. Pray for capacity suited to your tasks.

No man can live wrong and pray right. No man can pray right and live wrong.

God hears no more than the heart speaks.

I waited patiently for the Lord; and He inclined unto me, and heard my cry.   Ps. 40:1

Prayer should be the key of the morning and the bolt of the night.

People that do a lot of kneeling don't do much lying.

"Men may spurn our appeals, reject our message, oppose our arguments, despise our persons, but they are helpless against our prayers" said Sidlow Baxter.

The angel of the Lord encampeth round about them that fear Him, and delivereth them.

Ps. 34:7

Martin Luther: "I have so much to do (today) that I shall spend the first three hours in prayer."

MY PRAYER FOR THEE

The Lord preserve thy going out,
  The Lord preserve thy coming in;
God send His angels round about
  To keep thy soul from every sin,
And when thy going out is done,
  And when thy coming in is o'er,
When in death's darkness all alone,
  Thy feet can come and go no more,
The Lord preserve thy going out
  From this dark world of grief and sin,
While angels standing round about
  Sing— "GOD PRESERVE THY COMING IN!"

PREACHING

I preached as never sure to preach again, And as a dying man to dying men.

—Richard Baxter

The preacher does better
When you are there;
'Tis hard to preach
to an empty chair.

PROCRASTINATION

TIME BANK

Let's suppose that you had a bank that each morning credited your account with $1440, with one condition:

Whatever part you had failed to use during the day to be erased from your account—no balance to be carried over.

What would you do?

You'd draw out every cent every day and use it to the best advantage.

Well, you do have such a bank, and its name is TIME. Every morning it credits you with 1440 minutes. It rules off as forever lost whatever portion of this you have failed to invest to good purpose. Nor is there any drawing against tomorrow.

Tomorrow cannot be found on God's calendar.

Tomorrow sounds so innocent, but it is life's most dangerous word.

Tomorrow is the road that leads to the town called Never.

Tomorrow is the barred and bolted door that shuts people out of heaven.

Tomorrow is the nursemaid of hell.

Tomorrow is Satan's word. Those who expect to repent tomorrow usually die today. Don't count on tomorrow!

God has promised forgiveness to your repentance today, but not a tomorrow, so do not procrastinate.

Since our task is difficult, we dare not relax.
Since our opportunities are brief, we dare not delay.

Lost time is never found.

Use not today what tomorrow will need.

Postponed obedience is disobedience.

One can never catch up with good intentions.

Procrastination is soul suicide on the installment plan.

PROVIDENCE

The Lord was with Joseph. Gen. 39:2,21

Joseph might well wonder! He had experienced the pit, with its mire, darkness and horror. Then came slavery with life separation from loved ones, followed by the shameful scheming of Potiphar's wife, leading to an Egyptian jail, with its pollution and brutality. Must Joseph conclude, as his father once had done, "All these things are against me"? They might seem to be, but each bitter experience was but a link in the chain of events that led to that exalted place — supreme in Egypt. Truly, the Lord was with Joseph!

— F.W.S.

The saints should never be dismayed, nor sink in hopeless fear; For when they least expect His aid, the Savior will appear. This Abraham found: he raised his knife; God saw, and said, "Forbear! Yon ram shall yield his meaner life; behold the victim there." Once David seemed Saul's certain prey; Behold! Saul's foes at hand; Saul turns his arms another way, to save the invaded land. When Jonah sank beneath the wave, He thought to rise no more; But God prepared a fish to save, and bear him to the shore.

I said: "Let me walk in the field";
  God said: "Nay, walk in the town";
I said: "There are no flowers there";
  He said: "No flowers, but a crown."

I said: "But the sky is black,
  There is nothing but noise and din";
But He wept as He sent me back,
  "There is more," He said, "there is sin."

I said: "But the air is thick,
  And fogs are veiling the sun";
He answered: "Yet souls are sick,
  And souls in the dark undone."

I said: "I shall miss the light,
  And friends will miss me, they say";
He answered me, "Choose tonight,
  If I am to miss you, or they."

I pleaded for time to be given;
  He said: "Is it hard to decide?
It will not seem hard in heaven
  To have followed the steps of your Guide."

I cast one look at the fields,
  Then set my face to the town;
He said: "My child, do you yield?
  Will you leave the flowers for the crown?"

Then into His hand went mine,
  And into my heart came He;
And I walk in a light Divine,
  The path I had feared to see.

—George MacDonald

God always gives His best to those who leave the choice with Him

Now unto him that is able to keep you from falling, and to present you faultless before the presence of his glory with exceeding joy, to the only wise God our Saviour, be glory and majesty, dominion and power, both now and ever. Amen. **Jude 24, 25**

Within Thy circling power I stand;
On every side I find Thy hand;
Awake, asleep, at home, abroad,
I am surrounded still with God. —I. Watts

Blest proofs of power and grace divine that meet us in His Word;
May every deep felt care of mine be trusted with the Lord.
Wait for His seasonable aid, and though it tarry, wait:
The promise may be long delayed, but cannot come too late.
— Choice Gleanings

If some things were omitted, or altered, as we would,
The WHOLE might be unfitted to work for perfect good.
— Choice Gleanings

The dark threads are as needful in the Weaver's skillful hand,
As the threads of gold and silver in the pattern He has planned.

All of my life's "why's" and "when's" and "where's" and "wherefore's" are in God's hands. I need not question.

I know not the way He leads me, but well I know my Guide.
— Martin Luther

He who piloted the patriarch through the deluge, fed the prophet by the brook, supplied the widow's cruse, watched over the imprisoned apostles, and numbers every hair on our heads, is also the One who watches over us and says, "Let not your heart be troubled."

Able to keep! Yes, able to keep, rough though the path be — rugged and steep; tender the heart that is caring for me, mighty the grace, "sufficient for thee." Able to keep; my weakness He knows, strong the temptation, crafty the foes, God is my refuge, He is my shield: power of Almighty never shall yield. "Able to keep!" how sure is the word: He is my Keeper, Savior and Lord. "Never shall perish," one of His sheep, Glory to God! He is able to keep.

— Choice Gleanings

The STOPS of a good man are ordered of the Lord as well as his STEPS.

—George Mueller

In one thousand trials it is not five hundred of them that work for the believer's good, but nine hundred and ninety nine of them AND ONE BESIDE.

REGRET

SEVEN THINGS YOU WILL NEVER REGRET

Showing kindness to an aged person.
Destroying a letter written in anger.
Offering the apology that saves a friendship.
Stopping a scandal that was wrecking a reputation
Helping a boy find himself.
Taking time to show your mother consideration.
Accepting the judgment of God on any question.

RELIGION

A death-bed repentance at best is a weak and slender plank on which to trust one's all.	The religions of the world say, Do and Live. The religion of the Bible says, Live and Do.
Some people have too much religion to be happy at a ball game, but too little to be happy at a prayer meeting.	The man who is ashamed of his religion has a religion of which he ought to be ashamed.
Many people treat their religion as a spare tire — they never use it except in an emergency.	Some people's religion is like the old wheelbarrow — easily upset and must be pushed.

The religion of some people is well developed at the mouth, but lame at the hands and feet.

Some people have just enough religion to make them uncomfortable.
— John Wesley

A religion that
COSTS NOTHING
does nothing.

The world doesn't need a definition of religion as much as it needs a demonstration.

Your true religion is the life you live, not the creed you profess.

If you hold your religion lightly you are sure to let it slip.

Many people use religion like a bus—
they ride it only when it goes their way.

Still religion,
like still water,
is the first to freeze.

Religion is meant to be bread for our daily use, not cake for special occasions.

REPENTANCE

REPENTANCE is made up of three things:

1. There is a change of mind.
We wish to do good instead of wishing to do evil.

2. There is a change of heart.
Instead of loving sin we have now "set our affections on things above." We love Jesus Christ and His commandments. "O how love I thy law" (Ps. 119:97). This can never come about by an act of will, but only by an act of God. He gives us a "new heart" and a "new spirit" (Ezek. 18:31). We become "Partakers of the divine nature" (II Peter 1:4). And then "it is God which worketh in us both to will and to do of his good pleasure" (Phil. 2:13).

3. There is a change of life.
Thereby we show that our repentance is real and true.

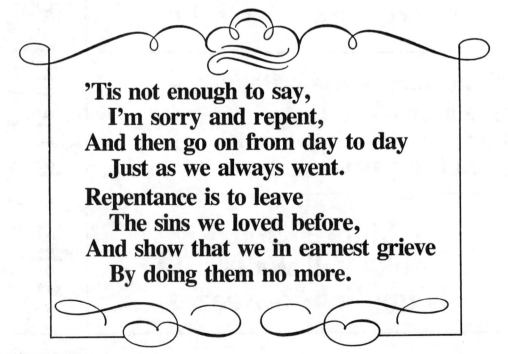

'Tis not enough to say,
 I'm sorry and repent,
And then go on from day to day
 Just as we always went.

Repentance is to leave
 The sins we loved before,
And show that we in earnest grieve
 By doing them no more.

REWARDS

**The crowns we will wear in heaven
must be won on earth.**

He who does good for good's sake
seeks neither praise nor reward,
but he is sure of both in the end.
— Penn

The
CROSSLESS
life
is a
CROWNLESS
death.

Favour is deceitful,
and beauty is vain;
but a woman that
feareth the Lord,
she is to be praised.
— Prov. 31:30

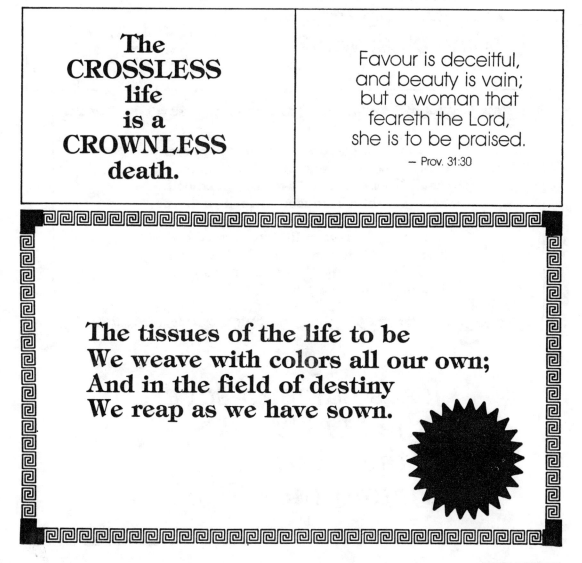

The tissues of the life to be
We weave with colors all our own;
And in the field of destiny
We reap as we have sown.

SALVATION

Salvation is FREE but stewardship is COSTLY.	Salvation may come QUIETLY, but we can't remain QUIET about it.
If Christ is the way, why waste time traveling some other way?	Christ BELIEVED is salvation RECEIVED.

"I'm afraid God will never accept me," said a poor woman in deep distress of soul. "He never will," was the unexpected answer, which caused a look of blank astonishment to cross the face of the woman. "He never will," repeated the visitor, "but He has accepted Christ. And by faith we can say, 'He hath made us accepted in the Beloved.'"

Jesus came to save the LOST, the LAST, and the LEAST.

D. L. Moody is said to have once returned from a meeting with a report of "two and one-half conversions." "I suppose you mean two adults and one child," said the man who was his host. "No," said Mr. Moody, "I mean two children and one adult. You see, the children can give their whole lives, but the adult only has half of his left to give." How true this is! Suppose that Paul would have been converted at 70 instead of 25. There would have been no Paul in history. There was a Matthew Henry because he was converted at the age of 11, and not at 70. There was a Jonathan Edwards because he was converted at eight and not at 80. And there was a Richard Baxter because he was converted at six instead of 60.

Notice the complete change of mind in the returning prodigal son (Luke 15). His father, once forsaken, is now his hope and desire. His home, once despised, is now like heaven to him. The lad, once so proud and self-satisfied, now knows himself unworthy to be called a son. The father's loving greeting, the kiss of forgiveness, the best robe, the feast are pictures of God's salvation.

Trembling, we had hoped for mercy—
Some lone place within His door;
But the crown, the throne, the mansion,
All were ready long before.
And in past and distant ages,
In those courts so bright and fair,
Ere we were, was He rejoicing,
All He won with us to share.

— Choice Gleanings

No sermon to unbelievers has any real value
that does not contain the three "R's"—
  RUINED by sin,
   REDEMPTION by Christ,
    REGENERATION by the Holy Spirit.

Many are on the salvation train,
but a lot of them are in the sleeping car.

**If we could merit our own salvation,
Christ would never have died to provide it.**

Believing Christ died, that's history.
Believing Christ died for you, that's salvation.

John 3:16 sends thousands to heaven.
Revelation 3:16 sends millions to hell.

The empty cross
and the empty tomb
speak of a
full salvation.

SATAN

Our flesh is the worm on the devil's hook.

The devil is willing for a person to
profess Christianity
as long as he does not
practice Christianity.

God put the church in the world.
Satan seeks to put the world in the church.

◆◆◆

The devil is never too busy
to rock the cradle of a
sleeping saint.

◆◆◆

The devil will extend plenty of credit,
but think of the payment.

◆◆◆

An IDLE person
is the devil's PLAYMATE.

◆◆◆

He who delays his repentance
pawns his soul with the devil.

One of the devil's snares is to occupy us with the past and future so as to take away our peace for the present.

The devil gratifies: God satisfies.

Pride is a master sin of the devil.

Satan is to be dreaded as a lion; More to be dreaded as a serpent; and most to be dreaded as an angel.

The devil has to work hard for what he gets in the home of a praying mother.

The devil uses a vacant mind as a dumping ground.

SERVICE

Believe there is nothing too small to do well.

When duty calls some people are never at home.

Be not simply good. Be good for something.

The believer's talents are not to be laid up for self but laid out in service.

Hard work, cheerfully done, is easy work. Light work, unwillingly done, is mere drudgery.	Service was never intended as a substitute for a godly life.
True service is love for Christ in working clothes.	No matter how small your lot may be in life, there is always room for a service station.

We are saved to serve, but we never serve to get saved.

HOW DO YOU GO?

There are three types of Christians who respond to the call to service.
1. Rowboat Christians—have to be pushed.
2. Sailboat Christians—always go with wind.
3. Steamboat Christians—make up their minds where they ought to go and go there regardless of wind and weather.

One who has a light view of sin never has great thoughts of God, because God hates sin.	The best way to know God's estimate of sin is to realize the tremendous price it took to atone for sin, the death of God's Son.
Use sin as it will use you; spare it not for it will not spare you.	**If sin would be better known, Christ would be better thought of.**
Whenever a man is ready to uncover his sins, God is always ready to cover them.	We need to ask the Lord to save us from evil hearing as well as from evil talking.
True repentance consists of the heart that is broken for sin and broken from sin.	**How candid we are in confessing other people's sin.**
Sin is the greatest of detectives: be sure your sin will find you out.	His heart cannot be pure whose tongue is not clean.
Christ is not sweet until sin is made bitter to us.	**If you do not want the fruits of sin, stay out of sin's orchard.**

Unless sin is confessed, it will fester.

Either give up sin or give up hope.

The wages of sin have never been reduced.

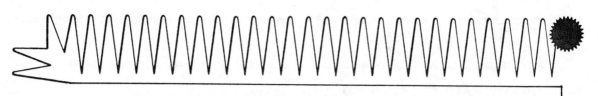

**Sin has many tools,
but a lie
is a handle that fits them all.**

Sin is its own detective.

Lying and stealing live next door to each other.

**Sin causes the Christian's cup of joy
to spring a leak.**

The backslider runs from the Lord
when he walks in his own way.

Few love to hear of the sins they love to act.

The bad thing about little sins is that they grow up so fast.

You hate sin just insofar as you love Christ.

Sin forsaken is the surest sign of sin forgiven.

The most expensive thing in the world is sin.

Sin may come upon thee by surprise,
but do not let it
dwell with thee as a guest.

SPEECH

People with sharp tongues often end up by cutting their own throats.

Profanity is the crutch of conversational cripples.

A GENTLEMAN NEVER SWEARS; HE HAS A BETTER VOCABULARY!

The less thunder, the gentler the rain.

Hot words make cool friendships.

You don't have to explain something you have not said.

A lot of things are opened by mistake, but none so often as the mouth.

The most untameable thing in the world has its den just back of the teeth.

It often shows a fine command of language to say nothing.

A lot of trouble in this world is caused by combining a narrow mind with a wide mouth.

They always talk who seldom think.

A wound from the tongue is worse than a wound from the sword.

He who knows much knows how to hold his tongue.

TRAINING

BRING YOUR SON UP OR DOWN
To Bring Down a Son

1. Let him have plenty of spending money.
2. Permit him to choose his own companions without restraint or direction.
3. Give him a latch-key and allow him to return home late at night.
4. Make no inquiry as to where and with whom he spends his leisure moments.
5. Give him to understand that manners make a good substitute for morals.
6. Teach him to expect pay for every act of helpfulness to others.
7. Let him spend Sunday hours, between services, on the street.
8. Be careful never to let him hear your voice in prayer for his salvation and spiritual growth.

To Bring Up a Son

1. Make home the brightest and most attractive place on earth.
2. Make him responsible for the performance of a limited number of daily duties.
3. Never punish him in anger.
4. Do not ridicule his conceits, but rather talk frankly on matters in which he is interested.
5. Let him feel free to invite his friends to your home and table.
6. Be careful to impress upon his mind that making character is more important than making money.
7. Live Christ before him all the time, then you will be able to talk Christ to him with power.
8. Be much in prayer for his salvation and spiritual growth.

God develops spiritual power in our lives through the shaping pressure of hard places.

Juvenile delinquency, a wise father said, is the result of parents trying to train children without starting at the bottom.

Train up a child in the way he should go and when he is old, he will not depart from it (Prov. 22:6).

The prevalence of juvenile delinquency is proving that some parents are not getting at the SEAT of the problem.

A little each day is much in a year.
A little explained, a little endured,
A little forgiven, the quarrel is cured.

You cannot lift your children to a higher level than that on which you live yourself.

It is unreasonable to expect a child to listen to your advice and ignore your example.

"This piece of marble", said a sculptor, "costs a thousand dollars. I careful ought to be with my chisel." "This bit of rosy clay", said a parent, "cost the precious blood of the REDEEMER. How careful ought I to be moulding it for Him."

SCHOOL DAYS
This life is a school of EDUCATION;
Each day brings forth a RECITATION.
Death ends the term without VACATION,
And then comes the final EXAMINATION.

Take care of your lambs, or where will you get your sheep from?
— Spurgeon

Building boys is better than mending men.

If we work on MARBLE, it will perish.
If we work on BRASS, time will efface it.
If we rear TEMPLES, they will crumble into dust.
But if we work on IMMORTAL MINDS; as we embue them with principles, with the just fear of God and love of our fellow men, we engrave on those tablets something that will brighten all ETERNITY.

—Daniel Webster

The best thing parents can spend on children is time, not money.

Education commences at the mother's knee and every word spoken in the hearsay of little children tends toward the formation of character.

When to Start
Ere a child has reached to SEVEN
Teach him all the way to heaven;
Better still the work will thrive
If he learns before he's FIVE.

— C. H. Spurgeon

One father is worth more than a hundred schoolmasters.

The school of suffering graduates rare students.

What should not be heard by little ears should not be said by big mouths.

Make the mistakes of yesterday your lessons for today.

It takes dedicated parents to produce consecrated children.

A switch in time saves crime.

ENVY—the seed sown.
STRIFE—the plant grown.

THANKSGIVING

TIME TO MOVE
Too many a discontented mourner
Is spending his days on GRUMBLE CORNER–
Sour and sad–whom I long to entreat
To get a house on THANKSGIVING STREET!

He enjoys much
who is thankful for little.

A grateful mind
is
both great and a happy mind.

Giving thanks always
FOR ALL THINGS. Eph. 5:20

Thanks to God for my Redeemer,
Thanks for all Thou dost provide,
Thanks for times now but a memory,
Thanks for Jesus by my side,
Thanks for pleasant, balmy springtime,
Thanks for dark and dreary fall,
Thanks for tears by now forgotten,
Thanks for peace within my soul,
Thanks for prayers that Thou hast answered.
Thanks for what Thou dost deny,
Thanks for storms that I have weathered,
Thanks for all Thou dost supply,
Thanks for pains, and thanks for pleasure,
Thanks for comfort in despair,
Thanks for grace that none can measure,
Thanks for love beyond compare,
Thanks for roses by the wayside,
Thanks for thorns their stems contain,
Thanks for home and thanks for fireside,
Thanks for hope, that sweet refrain,
Thanks for joy and thanks for sorrow,
Thanks for heavenly peace with Thee,
Thanks for hope in the tomorrow,
Thanks through all eternity.

Thank God for dirty dishes,
They have a tale to tell;
While others may go hungry
We've eaten very well.
With home, health and happiness
I shouldn't want to fuss,
By the stack of evidence
God's been very good to us!

TRIALS

When the storm is raging round thee,
Call on Me in humble prayer,
I will fold my arms around thee,
Guard thee with the tenderest care,
In the trial, I will make thy pathway clear.

Storms make a strong tree,
testings make a strong Christian.

God sends trials not to impair us,
but to improve us.

In times of affliction we commonly meet
the sweetest experiences of the love of God.

Take heart, believer,
the darker the night,
the nearer the dawn.

THE CONQUEROR

No matter how the storms may rage
   Upon the sea of life,
No matter how the waves may beat,
   No matter what the strife;
The Lord is just the same today
   As when He walked the sea,
And He can conquer every storm
   That life may send to thee.

The waves are raging everywhere
   And men are sore distressed,
But all they need is found in Him
   Who giveth perfect rest;
So cast your care upon the Lord
   Whose strength will never fail,
He calms the waves for your frail bark
   His power will e'er prevail.

No branch escapes the pruning knife;
No jewel the polishing wheel;
No child the correction rod;
No chosen vessel the thorn.

Great trials prepare for great service.

A smooth sea never made a skillful mariner.

**If you're taking a beating, cheer up;
God is just stirring the batter to bring you a blessing.**

TRUST

A pilot was experiencing difficulty in landing his plane because of fog; and the airport decided to bring him in by radar. As he began to receive directions from the ground he suddenly remembered a tall pole in the flight path, and appealed in panic to the control tower about it. The reply came bluntly, "You obey instructions; we'll take care of obstructions." How many a Christian hesitates to obey God's Word because of problems and difficulties! If we only obey, He is capable of dealing with the problems and difficulties.

What Thou today shalt provide,
Let me as a child receive;
What tomorrow may betide,
Calmly to Thy wisdom leave,
'Tis enough that Thou wilt care;
Why should I the burden bear?

The man that trusts God is the man that can be trusted.

Trust in the Lord with all thine heart; and lean not upon thine own understanding. In all thy ways acknowledge Him, and he shall direct your paths. Be not wise in thine own eyes: fear the Lord and depart from evil (Prov. 2:5-7).

Ask not HOW, but trust Him still;
Ask not WHEN, but wait His will;
SIMPLY ON HIS WORD RELY,
God SHALL all your need supply.

The fear of man bringeth a snare; whoso putteth his trust in the Lord shall be safe (Prov. 29:25).

COMMIT thy way unto the Lord; TRUST also in him, and he shall BRING IT TO PASS.
—Ps. 37:5

When we cannot see our way, let us trust and still obey;
He who bids us forward go, cannot fail the way to show,
Night with Him is never night, where He is there all is light,
When He calls us, why delay? They are happy who obey.

The Lord redeemeth the soul of His servants: and none of them that trust in Him shall be desolate.   Psalm 34:22

I'll never distrust my God for cloth or bread while the lilies flourish and the ravens are fed.

He who brought me hither will bring me hence; no other guide I need.

Trust in yourself, and you are doomed to disappointment.
Trust in your friends, and they will die and leave you.
Trust in your money, and you may have it taken from you.
Trust in reputation, and some slanderous tongue will blast it.
Trust in God, and you will never be confounded.

TRUTH

A man in the right with God on his side, is in the majority though he be alone.

Better be ignorant than to know too much that is not true.

Simplicity is truth's most becoming garb.

There is nothing so strong and safe in an emergency of life as the simple truth.

Without the WAY, there is no going;
Without the TRUTH, there is no knowing;
Without the LIFE, there is no living.

— Thomas a Kempis

Be bold in what you stand for,
but careful in what you fall for.

In quarreling, the truth is always lost.

Truth doesn't hurt—
unless it ought to.

Truth is not always popular,
but it is always right.

Truth has only to exchange hands
a few times to become fiction.

The truth is no less truth
because it cannot be explained.

Another good thing about telling the truth is you don't have to remember what you said.

WARNING

Noah's Carpenters

Many hundred years ago
   They ventured to remark
That Noah had some carpenters
   To help him build the Ark.
But sad to say on that last day
   When Noah entered in,
Those carpenters were left outside
   And perished in their sin.

How sad to think they may have
   Helped to build the Ark so great,
Yet still they heeded not God's Word
   And awful was their fate.
Today the same sad fate exists
   Among the sons of men, they
Help to build the so-called Church
   Who are not born again.

They stay behind for sacrament,
   They work, they sing, they pray;
Yet never have accepted Christ,
   The Life, the Truth, the Way.
Another judgment day will come,
   As sure as came the flood,
And only those will be secure
   Who shelter 'neath Christ's Blood.

Neglect your business and become bankrupt.
Neglect your health and be in your grave.
Neglect your fields and have no harvest.
NEGLECT YOUR SOUL and be DAMNED!

"I understand you and your wife are going to be separated," said a friend to a well-known judge. "How dare you insinuate any such thing?" shouted the judge, his face purple with anger. "My wife and I love each other very much."

"Is that so?" queried the friend. "Well, I heard from your doctor that she has only a short time to live, and since I know she is a Christian she will go to be with the Lord. Where are you going when you die?"

The judge stood awhile quietly thinking. His face began to pale as the words took effect. He cried out. "My God, save me. All these years I have been turning away from Thee. Forgive me God and save me."

The man who trims himself to suit everybody will soon whittle himself away.	**The high cost of living is nothing compared to the high cost of sinning.**
To lose one's wealth is much, To lose one's health is more, To lose one's soul is such a loss, as nothing can restore.	He that loveth pleasure shall be a poor man: he that loveth wine and oil shall not be rich. (Prov. 21:17).
When you jump at conclusions you can't always expect a happy landing.	**To lose all for Christ is my best gain; and to gain all without Him would be my worst loss.**
An evil thought passes through your door first as a stranger; then it enters as a guest, and then it installs itself as a master.	Between dreaming of tomorrow and regretting yesterday there's little time left doing anything today.

I am only a small cigarette.
I am not much of a mathematician,
But I can ADD to a person's nervous trouble.
I can SUBTRACT from his physical energy.
I can MULTIPLY his aches and pains.
I take INTEREST from his work,
And DISCOUNT chances for success.

The moving finger writes; and having writ,
Moves on; nor all the piety nor wit
Shall lure it back to cancel half a line,
Nor all your tears wash out a word of it.

It's not what you eat that causes ulcers;
it's what's eating you.

MIRROR

One day a rich man of a miserly disposition
visited a rabbi, who took him by the hand
and led him to a window. "Look out there,"
he said. The rich man looked out into the
street. "What do you see?" "I see men and
women and children." Again the rabbi took
him to a mirror. "What do you see now?" "I
see myself." Then the rabbi said, "Behold,
the window there is glass and the mirror is
glass also. But the glass of the mirror is
covered with silver. No sooner is silver
added than you cease to see others and see
only yourself."

There are no infidels in eternity and very few on death-beds. Take heed!

Those are marked to ruin who are deaf to reproof and good counsel.

The best way to wipe out a friendship is to sponge on it.

The pleasures of sin are for a season; but its wages are eternal.

As a moth gnaws a garment, so covetousness consumes a man's spirituality.

He who cannot forgive others breaks the bridge over which he himself must pass.

A man's reputation is only what men think him to be; his character is what God knows him to be.

The measure of a man's real character is what he would do if he knew he would never be found out.

He that being often reproved hardeneth his neck, shall suddenly be destroyed, and that without remedy (Prov. 29:1).

Whoso stoppeth his ears at the cry of the poor, he also shall cry himself but shall never be heard (Prov. 12:13).

It is easy to give another a piece of your mind, but when you are through, you may have lost your peace of mind.

If you want to enter a real race, just let a few bills run, and try to catch up with them.

If you are not as close to God as you once were, you need not wonder who it is who moved.

What you laugh at tells plainer than words what you are.

Beware, Christian, of three things: doubt, dirt, and debt.

To every man opens a high way and a low way and every man decides the way that he shall go.

The real problem of your leisure is how to keep other people from using it.

A Scottish shepherd was once asked if his sheep would follow the voice of a stranger. He replied: "Yes, when they are sick, but never when they are well. A sick sheep will follow anybody." No wonder false shepherds get quite a following in these Laodicean days!

Say it with flowers,
Say it with mink,
But never, Oh, never
Say it with ink!

Life, like a mirror, never gives back
more than we put into it.

Boys flying kites, haul in their white-winged birds;
You can't do this when you are flying words.
"Careful with fire" is good advice, we know.
"Careful with words" is ten times doubly so.
Thoughts unexpressed, may sometimes fall back dead;
But God Himself can't kill them, when they are sped.

— E. D. Hooey

From a little spark may burst a mighty flame.	Never was there good or ill done that did not produce its like.
What you are in the sight of God, that you really are.	**A man may be almost saved yet entirely lost.**
When you turn "green" with envy, you're getting "ripe" for trouble.	It is easier to learn truth than to unlearn error.
A loose tongue often gets a person in a tight place.	**Yesterday's unfinished task is a mortgage on today.**
If you want to be miserable, HATE somebody.	People who fly in a rage always make a bad landing.

The clock of life is wound but once
And no man has the power
To tell just when the hands will stop—
At late or early hour.
NOW is the only time you own;
Live, love, toil with a will—
Place no faith in TOMORROW for
The clock may then be still.

Bad habits are like a
comfortable bed—
easy to get into,
but hard to get out of.

These six things the Lord hates: yea, seven are an abomination unto him: a proud look, a lying tongue, and hands that shed innocent blood, a heart that deviseth wicked imaginations, feet that be swift in running mischief, a false witness that speaks lies, and he that soweth discord among brethren (Prov. 6:16-19).

I have only just a minute,
just sixty seconds in it;
forced upon me—
 can't refuse it,
  didn't seek it,
   didn't choose it.
I must suffer
 if I lose it;
give account
 if I abuse it;
just a tiny little minute
but eternity is in it.

Don't speak unless
You can improve
On the silence!

Before you give anyone a piece of your mind;
You ought to make sure, that you can get by with
What you might have left!

No man has a good enough memory to make a successful liar.	Never do what you cannot ask Christ to bless.
It is better not to be born than not to be born again.	Collapse in the Christian life is seldom a blowout; it is usually a slow leak. — Little
Crooked rivers get that way by following the line of least resistance. So do some people.	People who run into debt usually have to crawl out.

OUR WORDS
May hide our thoughts
BUT OUR ACTIONS
Will reveal them.

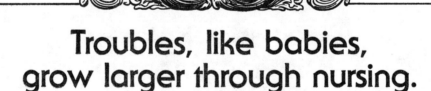

Troubles, like babies,
grow larger through nursing.

Four things come not back:
the spoken word,
  the sped arrow,
    the past life,
      and the neglected opportunity

Enter not into the path of the wicked, and go not in the way of evil men. Avoid it, pass not by it, turn from it, and pass away (Prov. 4:14, 15).

AN EXCELLENT RULE
TO FOLLOW IS—
If you can't write it
and sign it,
DON'T SAY IT!

Hot arguments have a way of producing cold shoulders.

I've a soul to be saved — may this truth be engraved
In my mind and my heart while I'm young;
O how awful the cost — if my soul should be lost,
And I die in my sins without Christ.

Behold the Lamb, the mighty Lamb with angry eyes aflame,
Coming to judge the sons of men who once blasphemed His name.
The mighty monarchs of the earth before Him speechless fall;
Behold the Lamb who conquered death, for He is Lord of all.

— F. H. Sterne

If you speak in anger, you will probably make the best speech you will ever regret.

Where death finds you,
There eternity will keep you.

The bow too tensely strung
is easily broken.

If you think you have no faults,
that makes one more.

Great haste makes waste.

— B. Franklin

The path of the world seems pleasant enough—
if you don't stop to think where you're going.

Hurry is the mother of most mistakes.

That which is unsaid may be said;
that which is said cannot be unsaid.

**Thoughts
are the
SEEDS
of future
DEEDS.**

**The longer one carries a grouch
the heavier it gets.**

Unless there is within us
that which is above us,
we shall soon yield
to that which is about us.

Scrapping will reduce
anything to scraps.

What must I do to be lost? NOTHING!
If you are not a believer, you are lost already.

Those who live in a WORRY
Invite death in a HURRY.

Do it now! Today will be yesterday tomorrow.	**The worst wheel on the cart makes the most noise.**

When alone, we have our own thoughts to watch;
when in the family, our tempers;
when in society, our tongues.

Nothing cooks your goose quicker than a boiling temper.

Sorrow makes us bitter or better.

Think that day lost whose low descending sun,
views from your hands no noble action done.

LOST YESTERDAY: somewhere between sunrise and sunset, two golden hours, each set with sixty diamond minutes. No reward is offered, for they are gone forever.

WEALTH

BUILDING OUR OWN MANSION

There is a legend of a wealthy woman who, when she reached heaven, was shown a very plain mansion. She objected. "Well," she was told, "that is the house prepared for you." "Whose is that fine mansion across the way?" she asked. "It belongs to your gardener." "How is it that he has one so much better than mine?" "The houses here are prepared from the materials that are sent up. We do not choose them, you do that by your earthly faithfulness."

(This may be a legend, but it bears a profound truth.)

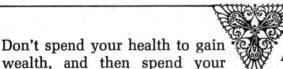

Don't spend your health to gain wealth, and then spend your wealth to regain health.

A good wife and health are a man's best wealth.

There are two ways of being rich. The one is to have all you want. The other is to be satisfied with what you have.

Fulfilment of our duties adds far more to our wealth than insistence on our rights.

A little house well FILLED,
A little field well TILLED,
A little wife well WILLED,
Are GREAT RICHES.

The poorest man is he whose only wealth is MONEY

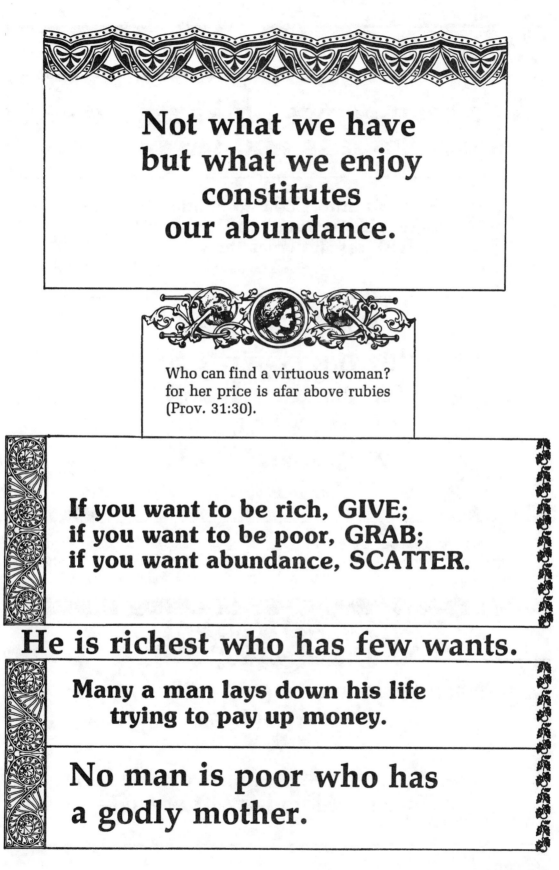

Not what we have
but what we enjoy
constitutes
our abundance.

Who can find a virtuous woman?
for her price is afar above rubies
(Prov. 31:30).

If you want to be rich, GIVE;
if you want to be poor, GRAB;
if you want abundance, SCATTER.

He is richest who has few wants.

Many a man lays down his life
trying to pay up money.

No man is poor who has
a godly mother.

WISDOM

As a man grows older and wiser, he talks less and says more.

He who shall introduce into public affairs the principles of primitive Christianity, will revolutionize the world.

— Benjamin Franklin

He is no fool who parts with that he cannot keep, to get that which he shall not lose.

The fruit of the righteous is a tree of life; and he that winneth souls is wise (Prov. 11:30).

He that is slow to wrath is of great understanding; but he that is hasty in spirit exalteth folly (Prov. 14:19).

When a wise man argues with a woman, he says nothing.

The educated may require knowledge, but true wisdom is a gift of God.

**A wise old owl lived in an oak,
The more he saw, the less he spoke;
The less he spoke, the more he heard,
Why can't we be like that old bird?**

Second thoughts are ever wiser.

**To admit I have been wrong is but saying that
I am wiser today than I was yesterday.**

Go to the ant thou sluggard; consider her ways and be wise; which having no guide, overseer, or ruler, provideth her meat in the summer, and gathereth her food in the harvest (Prov. 6:6-8).

Forethought is better than repentance.

The sum of wisdom is that the time is never lost that is devoted to work.

— Ralph Waldo Emerson

*Only one life,
'twill soon be past,
only what's done for Christ
will last.*

**We learn wisdom from failure
much more than from success.**

WORLDLINESS

THE WAY OUT

Philosophy says:
THINK your way out;

Indulgence says:
DRINK your way out;

Science says:
INVENT your way out;

Industry says:
WORK your way out;

Communism says:
STRIKE your way out;

Fascism says:
BLUFF your way out;

Militarism says:
FIGHT your way out;

The world says:
ENTERTAIN your way out;

But CHRIST says:
I AM the WAY out!

The more we are transformed by the power of Christ, the less we will be conformed to this world.

The wise men of Jesus' day presented frankincense. The worldly wise of our day present rank nonsense.

WORLDLINESS

"FOR ALL THAT IS IN THE WORLD—
The lust of the flesh — SENSUALITY
The lust of the eyes — MATERIALISM
And the pride of life — EGOTISM
IS NOT OF THE FATHER, BUT IS
OF THE WORLD."

I John 2:16

The more of heaven there is in our lives, the less of earth we shall covet.

You can't "wait on the Lord" and "run with the devil" at the same time.

The path of the world seems pleasant enough if you don't stop to think where you're going.

With such a starting point as the cross and such a goal as the Lord's coming, how can a Christian love the things of the world, the flesh, and the devil?

Chasing after pleasure is a confession of an unsatisfied life.

Lie down with dogs and you'll get up with fleas.

FOR THOSE WHO SAY, "I DON'T SEE ANY HARM IN IT."

1. Is the dust of worldiness in your eyes?
2. Would you accept it for your death-bed solace?
3. Is it consistent with, "The world is crucified unto me and I unto the world."?
4. Can you commune with God as freely after indulging in it?
5. Can you look to God for a blessing in the midst of it?
6. How will it appear at the Judgment Seat of Christ at His coming?

If your answers are negative, it must be wrong, and you'd be wise to take another course!

Your iniquities have separated between you and your God. Isa. 59:2

The moon in an eclipse complained to the sun, "Why dost thou not shine on me as usual?" "I am shining as I always do," the sun replied, "but the earth has got between us." And you, Christian, who have lost the joy of your salvation, and no longer bask in the sunshine of God's countenance, is it the earth and its pursuits that have come between your soul and Him, or what is it? He is the same, His love is as great as ever.

—Choice Gleanings

Some people have heaven on the tongue's end but the world on their fingertips.

Farewell, vain world;
My soul bids you adieu;
My Savior taught me
To abandon you.
Your charms may gratify
A sensual mind,
But cannot please
A soul for God designed.

— David Brainerd 1742

The more of heaven there is in our lives,
the less of earth we shall covet.

WORRY

**You can't change the past,
but you ruin a perfectly good present
by worrying about the future.**

Worry comes through
human interference
with the divine plan.

Why worry when you can pray?

It is only the fear of God that can deliver us from the fear of men.

An old man was asked what had most robbed him of joy in his life. His reply was, "Things that never happened."

Dr. Charles Mayo said: "I've never known a man who died of hard work, but many who die of worry."

Worry is interest paid on trouble before it is due.

If your all is in the hand of the Lord, why worry about what "they say"?

Worry is like a rocking chair; it will give you something to do but it won't get you anywhere.

The eagle that soars near the sun is not concerned how it will cross the raging stream.

Fear is unbelief parading in disguise.

Fear and faith cannot keep house together. When one enters, the other departs.

Nothing can make a trusting Christian blue.